HERITAGE BUILDERS

SOMEDAY I'M GONNA RENT THIS TOWN

EVEN STEVENS

HERITAGE BUILDERS PUBLISHING
MONTEREY, CLOVIS CALIFORNIA

HERITAGE BUILDERS PUBLISHING
©2015 by Even Stevens

First Edition 2015

Contributing Editor, Mason Smith
Cover Design, Rae House Creative Marketing
Book Design, Keith Bennett
Published by Heritage Builders Publishing
Clovis, California 93619
www.heritagebuilders.com   1-800-397-8267
ISBN 978-1-941437-92-6

Printed and bound in the United States of America.

To Seth and Luke,
my dear and brilliant sons.

TABLE OF CONTENTS

Someday I'm Gonna Rent This Town

ACKNOWLEDGMENTS

....

Even Stevens

To my wife, Korene, who believed in this book and hounded me through the years to get it done, always with love in her heart.

To Sherman Smith, who saw me play my songs in Muscle Shoals, walked up to me and stated, "I'm publishing a book on you!" What gifts he gave . . . a book! . . . and a friend. Thanks Sherm.

Eddie Rabbitt . . . Who knows how it all would have played out without you and your great talent. Here's to hundreds of songs and thousands of laughs and the best of times . . . I miss you my friend.

Jim Malloy and David Malloy . . . Teaming up with you gave me direction and your friendship and encouragement was invaluable and so inspiring. Thanks for always believing in me.

Mom, Dad and sister Sandy . . . always on my side.

Someday I'm Gonna Rent This Town

....

Duane Allen
Lead Singer, The Oak Ridge Boys

Life is full of clichés. They say it's not what you know, but who you know, and that old saying could never be more true than in The Oak Ridge Boys' career. Like most artists, it has been songwriters, publishers, and influential business people who have helped plot the path of our success. One of those special people, Even Stevens, keeps showing up regularly and in many different roles.

In fact, Even has shown up regularly in a lot of artists' careers. As a songwriter, he practically wrote Eddie Rabbit's entire award-winning discography; a list that's laden heavy with both pop and country radio smashes. While he was at it, he also penned million-selling singles and album tracks for internationally renowned acts like Dr. Hook, Kenny Rogers, Julio Iglesias, and Tim McGraw — to name only a few.

If you work on Music Row and you haven't met Even Stevens or recorded one of his hundreds of award-winning songs, you most likely have it on your bucket list. The Oak Ridge Boys met him years ago about the same time that he — and we — started making a little "noise" on the Nashville music scene in the late 1970's or early 1980's.

Since that time, we've recorded a number of our albums at

Emerald Sound, which is the premier Music Row recording studio that Even helped build. We also had the privilege of taking one of the songs he published and penned, "No Matter How High," to the top of the Billboard charts. It's one of three Even Stevens' songs we've recorded so far.

Even has had songs included in major motion pictures, and he's written well-known national commercial jingles. He's also produced albums by mainstream acts like Engelbert Humperdinck, Hillary Kanter, and Stella Parton. He's now a celebrated radio personality.

Speaking of clichés, I've always heard that you should never judge a book by its cover. Well, you shouldn't judge it by its title either. When Even Stevens writes that he might one day "rent" Nashville, don't believe a word of it. He already owns this town, lock, stock, and barrel.

I hope you'll enjoy his story. I'm honored that he asked me to play a small part in it.

SOMEDAY I'M GONNA RENT THIS TOWN

CHAPTER 1

....

Antigua, British West Indies 1979

It was a hot August day and you could hear the sound of sun-tan lotion bottles farting up and down the beach. There I lounged, slathered in coconut oil, a bronzed god with piña colada in hand, and a big 'ole *hit record* in every civilized country of the world with my song, *When You're In Love With A Beautiful Woman*. Ah, life was sweet indeed . . . but I digress.

The Beginning

I was born at Christ Hospital in Cincinnati, Ohio, son of a soldier just back from the Philippines and World War Two. My dad Floyd was a real character and a jack of all trades. After the war he worked selling soap to department stores, traveled and sang in a Scottish musical troupe, attended art college, and studied voice and opera at the Cincinnati Conservatory of Music. He later worked for Lou Miller Amusements in Indian Lake, Ohio, installing and repairing slot machines, pinballs, and jukeboxes. Our garage was always full of those machines and my sister, Sandy, and I would take the old 78 rpm records and break them up with a hammer and reassemble them like jigsaw puzzles. I'd take the steel balls from the pinball machines and sell them at school as "steelies," primo marbles. Later, dad became a Methodist minister, then an ordained Baptist minister, basically doing whatever was necessary to support a wife and two children. My dad was a straight shooter of high moral values.

My dad's father, Floyd Noel Stevens, a young man during the

30's, enlisted in the Armed Services to fight in World War One, three different times under three different names. Twice in the Army and once in the Navy. He won a Purple Heart once and an Oak Leaf Cluster for being wounded again. He was also a man of many talents. After the war he and his brother Earl sang in a Franklin Delano Roosevelt WPA vaudeville troupe, and grandpa later became an award winning salesman for the Wearever Aluminum Cookware Company. I still have all his trophies for leading the nation in sales. He also ran a printing press in Pennsylvania, sang in Chief Nemo's Scotch Highlanders and was a world-class fisherman. He didn't suffer fools easily nor care what too many people thought of him, good or bad. We took many summers off together, heading in his big old Buick for some secret fishing hole on some distant river he had discovered in his young years, usually in Pennsylvania or the Catskills. It was always a low-rent trip with grandpa. He cut a piece of plywood that he balanced on the back of the front seat and the rear back window deck, and that's where he slept each night, with me up in the front seat. He would chain smoke unfiltered Kools with the windows closed until he fell asleep, and in the morning I would wake up with my mouth so dry that my tongue would be stuck to the roof of my mouth. When it was lunchtime, we would pull into some little burg and stop at the first church he saw. He'd take his card table and camp stools from the trunk and we'd eat baked beans cold from the can. I remember being embarrassed one such day, when the congregation filed out of the church on a Sunday, and there I was, eating baked beans with grandpa in his specks, by the front steps calmly reading the paper.

My mom was a Kentucky girl whose alcoholic father was shot dead in front of her in a domestic confrontation with police when she was only 13, leaving her and her mother to raise two younger brothers, my uncles Jack and Ray. Opal went to work at thirteen and never stopped working her whole life. What a beauty; she was a sweetheart.

My mom worked as a waitress in a local truck stop called the Tip Top, in Bellefontaine, Ohio, where I, when I wasn't in school, spent the days sitting on stools by the pinball machines, watching the truck drivers rack up games and cash them in for real money, even though I believe such a thing was illegal in Ohio at the time. One fellow used to come in to eat and flirt with Mom and tip her with a pound of sausage from a cooler in his car trunk. That fellow was a young man named Bob Evans, who later started the huge Bob Evans chain of restaurants. The truckers gave me quarters to play the jukebox, and the first song I ever fell in love with was *This Old House* by Stuart Hamblen. I played it at least once every day one summer.

Mom worked hard to support us while my dad studied at Ohio Northern University. He preached at three churches in the mid-Ohio region, and we lived in the parsonage in the little burg of Marseilles. My earliest memories of that town were not so good. For some reason, there were folks there who downright disliked the preacher and his family. One night some juvenile delinquents castrated our family dog and left him on our front porch to bleed to death. My dad went to the town square to confront the suspected teens, and told everyone in earshot that only sick, gutless degenerates would ever do such a thing to a helpless animal.

On another occasion, my father was holding a Wednesday night prayer meeting at the church when the old lady across the street, Olgabee Essex, came running through the door screaming that her husband was having a heart attack. My father ran to her house and began resuscitating him until the ambulance arrived. For weeks after that incident my father caught holy hell from some of the congregation because he left the prayer meeting to help someone who wasn't a member of our church. Even at the age of seven I knew that they were way off base. I am sorry to say, things like that and other traumas associated with being a preacher's kid really turned me off to the organized side of religion throughout my life.

At an early age I became intrigued with my dad's record collection. He had albums by Tommy and Jimmy Dorsey and Buddy Clark, a great singer who died young in an airplane crash, crazy Spike Jones with Ish Kabibel singing *All I Want For Christmas Is My*

Two Front Teeth, and scores of 78 rpm records. One day I asked dad why there was a name in parenthesis under every song title, and he informed me that it was the name of the songwriter. Until then, I mistakenly thought, like most folks, that the singer wrote the song. After learning that gem of information, I never looked at another record without checking who wrote it. Magic names like Hoagie Carmichael, Julie Styne, and Sammy Cahn . . . it took me away to visions of them sitting in Hollywood at an upright piano, composing away. During my first and second grade days, my dad, uncle Bob, and sister Sandy would gather in the parsonage living room and record a weekly gospel music radio show for a local station, and I got the incredible job of starting and stopping the Wilcox Gay reel to reel tape recorder, then get the thrill of hearing the end product on the radio on Sunday afternoons. I was a recording engineer!

Uncle Bob was an electronics nut and built a theremin from radio parts and a yardstick. It was a ball messing with that weird sound. One day this really nervous old lady came by for her weekly therapy session with dad. Somebody had left the theremin power on and as she opened the door it made its signature sci-fi Frankenstein sound, and she immediately ran out the door in fear. My dad had to chase her out and calm her down.

We finally left Marseilles and moved to another small Ohio town by the name of Lewistown. There is a large metal historical sign on the edge of town stating that it was named after a Captain John Lewis who, on that spot, took an Indian woman dredge, (whatever that is, it doesn't sound good to me), for his own and settled down. Lewistown proved to be a kinder place to live. We bought a deserted cottage there that needed the kitchen floor jacked up out of the mud and extensive rehab before we could move in. My father and mother did all the work themselves, with the assistance of this eleven year old, and we settled down as the new preacher's family. Lewistown was a tiny village of about two hundred, so tiny that we only had one stoplight in the center of town, but it was eventually removed due to lack of use. There was a town pump for everyone's use in case any of our wells went dry. The commercial businesses in town consisted of Robson's general store, Shultz's two pump gas station, a grain elevator, and my mom's beauty shop, the Cut n Curl, located in the front of our home. In later years, my sister Sandy also got her beautician's license and worked side by side with my mother. Every woman in town came to have their hair permed, colored and styled by my mom, Opal. The Cut n Curl was a beehive of feminine activity and I could hear the chatter and smell of permanent wave solution through the walls in our living room.

Meanwhile, my father got tired of just getting by on a preacher's pittance and delved into other ways to make money. He opened a shoe repair shop in nearby Bellefontaine, sold Chicago Technical College courses in drafting, became a regional insurance salesman for New York Life and Prudential, and scouted the mid-west finding potential gas station property for the Ashland Oil Company. My sister, Sandy and my father began performing as The Gospel Balladeers, with Sandy on organ and my father doing the singing. They also began distributing courses on Christian music and Bible study to inmates of prisons and called their organization The Victory Institute. Along the way dad got disillusioned with the Methodist church and left to become an ordained Baptist minister, taking over a church in nearby DeGraff, Ohio. After ten years of preaching there, he bought the town's defunct movie theater and began The Victory Tabernacle, he and my sister ministering in words and music to whomever showed up. But perhaps my father's greatest achievement was becoming one of America's most knowledgeable authorities on piano rebuilding and tuning. He wrote two books on those subjects while serving as the President of the Piano Technicians Guild of America. Both books, published by Nelson-Hall, are still considered the go-to books on Piano Tuning in the world.

All in all my memories of life in Lewistown are idyllic and as similar to Mayberry RFD as they could possibly be. I rode my horse Rusty to school when the weather was nice and tied him under a big maple tree that I could see from my homeroom, though I'm sure that didn't help my habitual day dreaming one little bit. At lunch time I would ride him the three blocks home for Campbell's soup and grilled cheese, then back to my afternoon classes. My good friend was Stevie Jenkins, whose dad, Lou, owned the leather shop and the Diamond J. Donkey Basketball Company. He would book high schools where they pitted the student athletes against the faculty in basketball and baseball games, all played on the backs of donkeys with rubber shoes. When I got into my teen years, Stevie and I would accompany him on gigs and be the guys who ran around behind the donkeys, zapping their asses with battery powered shockers to make them buck and, hopefully, throw their riders. Lou was a rough cob of a guy. He was tall and stringy like Gary Cooper, always with a cigarette dangling from his mouth. He would have smoked chains if he could've lit them, and always had his hand in a number of things. He owned a beautiful palomino stallion named King that he hired out for breeding and periodically loaned to Hollywood cowboy star, Johnny Mack Brown, to use in parades and movies when the actor worked east of the Mississippi . . . I as understood it, Johnny Mack had an identical horse he used out west in California.

Lou also had a friend named Abe Martin who owned "Jimmy, The Roller Skating Horse." He trained that horse to roller skate with specially made skates on his hooves. Jimmy appeared on The Ed Sullivan Show and other national shows, and Lou would book them at roller skating rinks across America. Jimmy was Ohio Famous for a time, and that was fun for our little town.

I spent most weekends at local horse shows entering my horse into keg races, pickup races, and trail class competitions . . . that is, until I turned sixteen and discovered cars. My first car was a '53 Plymouth that I decked out with blue lights in the wheel wells, madras seat covers, and fur dice hanging from the rearview mirror. My first full fledged sexual experience involved a girl named Kate, in the backseat of that car, in a cemetery. I lasted a good minute, and she loved it so much that all the way back to her house she babbled on about how "we should get married now" and that this was "true love" if ever there was one. All I could think about as I drove back to my parents' house was "God, please make it that she don't have a disease or something."

Someday I'm Gonna Rent This Town

CHAPTER 2

....

Oh Dem Golden Slippers!

Every year the adults would put on a minstrel show at our high school, and my dad was always a big hit. We're talking the early 60's, and things were different then. He would smear black grease paint on his face, wear a big loud, baggy gold-sequined zoot suit and floppy hat and come out from the wings to meet another "black" man center stage to tell a joke . . . Amos & Andy style. My uncle Bob would tap dance and play drums and harmonica, Bert and Lavida Martin would perform on his jazz guitar and her accordion, and this weird woman would play *Indian Love Call* on the xylophone and everybody would applaud and laugh their white asses off, so happy that they could experience "negro" culture first hand. The only *real* black man within seventy-five miles of Lewistown was the blacksmith who nailed shoes on my horse. Needless to say, the minstrel shows didn't last past 1964, what with civil rights legislation and so on. But, honestly, people just didn't see anything wrong with those kind of shows in those days . . . as I said, things were different then.

Today I feel uncomfortable just watching the black choir that invariably appears on stage for the big finale at almost every country music award show on television. I can't help but think it's still an attempt to relive the minstrel days, keep alive and apologize for, in some strange way, that weird part of American history.

One night, when I was 16, it was just my father and I traveling through Mississippi on our way to Florida, when news came on the car radio that civil-rights activist, Medgar Evers had been killed.

My Dad & Grandpa as The Scotch Highlanders

We stopped for gas in some little town and this big fat redneck man came out of the station and said, "Hear what happened to that nigger Medgar Evers?" My dad looked him in the eye and replied, "Yea, someone shot him right in the back." We had a nervous ride for the next hour or so with my dad checking the rearview mirror for the Ku Klux Klan every couple of miles. Years later I realized the guts that took on my dad's part, and I've always been proud of him for that reaction and other things he got right.

Rewind:

For instance, there was a cowgirl who lived on the edge of town who could outride any guy in the county . . . JoAnn Godwin was her name. She was tough as nails, and broke and sold horses for a living. When I first got interested in horses, she arranged for my dad to buy a gorgeous pinto named Pepper. It had identical black and white makings on each side of it's body and was a beauty, though I should have known by it's name, right off, that I was in for trouble.

JoAnn spent a few weeks breaking in that horse and assured us that it was ready to ride. Every time I got on Pepper he threw me to the ground. I was only eleven or so and couldn't handle it, so my dad sold Pepper. Later on we found out he became the Grand Champion Show Pony of Ohio.

JoAnn loved all us kids in town and when we wanted to start a little league baseball team, no one was interested in setting it up or coaching us, so JoAnn took on the job. After our team won a few games and people started coming to them, some of the men in our little town decided it was time to take over and started a movement to oust JoAnn as coach. They had a big town meeting at the school one night to do just that, and their excuse was "what if one of the boys gets hit with a baseball in the testicles . . . is JoAnn gonna rush out on the field and help him?" My Dad spoke up and told them all that if that ever happened, he and other fathers would come to the rescue and that they were all a "bunch of jerks" for trying to take the team away from the lady who cared enough to start the team in the first place. Well, of course, they ended up getting their way and breaking JoAnn's big heart anyhow. I remember, as a kid, thinking, "Hey, if I got hit in the nuts, I'd sure rather have a girl look at 'em than some dude!"

Someday I'm Gonna Rent This Town

CHAPTER 3

....

Ahh, Sweet Music!

My first true musical awakening happened in 1963. I was driving home from a date around midnight in my '53 Plymouth listening to WOWO in Fort Wayne, Indiana. Following some Mitch Miller sing-along-song, the radio virtually came alive. I pulled over to the side of the road, rolled down the windows and turned it up to "11." The song was *Love Me Do* by the Beatles and it put a smile all over my body. After hearing *Love Me Do*, I gave up on haircuts, doing the Twist, and wearing penny loafers. For the junior prom I shunned the rented tuxedo and wore a baby blue collarless Beatles jacket, skinny tie, Beatle boots and pegged pants. The school principal soon started noticing my shaggy-ass hair, and the teachers, my definite lack of interest.

1964 was an uneventful year except for what was happening on the radio. Of course the Beatles were everywhere and their influence spread over the airwaves like a friendly virus. Out with the old and in with the Mersey Beat. It was an exciting time.

Someday I'm Gonna Rent This Town

CHAPTER 4

Barber College

After graduating from high school, I decided to become a barber and enrolled at the Dayton Barber College. Some college! It was located on 5th street, the sleaziest street in downtown Dayton, inhabited by winos, weirdos, and dangerous derelicts. I actually walked up on the aftermath of a murder one evening. My first day, they handed me a barber's kit complete with electric clippers, combs, shears, soap and mug, and a straight razor, then gave a twenty minute demonstration on shaving and told us to "get out there and get to work." I wielded that straight razor and shaved an intoxicated old man within two hours of walking through that door. I only drew blood six or seven times, but that was considered promising, so they let me stay. Oh, I forgot to mention . . . he pissed in my chair. An instructor ordered me to clean it up and I refused, pointing out that I paid *them* to attend their "college," not the other way around. I suggested that they hire a janitor for such jobs. That incident labeled me as a trouble maker to the faculty and set the tone for my entire stay in those hallowed halls.

It was there that I heard my first barber jokes. A man is sitting in a barber chair and the barber says, "Mr. Johnson, you've got kind hair . . . the kind I'd like to spit in," or, "Mr. Johnson, you've got wavy hair. One side stands up and waves at the other!" or, "would you like those ears on or off?"

Now, it may sound strange that a Beatle-freak would choose to become a barber, but my best friend Jerry McLaughln was a barber, and I thought he lived a very cool life. Jerry was a few years older than me, but took me under his wing just like a big brother. It was he who turned me on to the greats of early rock and roll like Roy Orbison, Buddy Holly, and Elvis. He lived just down the street from me and let me hang out after school and weekends, and we wore his records out. Jerry always had the sharpest cars and dated the prettiest women, and sometimes he'd let me tag along in those days before I was old enough to drive myself. I really looked up to Jerry, so I suppose that's the reason I became a barber. Some of my fondest memories revolve around us cruising down the Ohio back roads at night in his convertible, with a far-off Chicago radio station playing songs like James Brown's *Oh Baby Don't You Weep*. Jerry moved on to other professions in his life, but remains my best friend to this very day. He's such a solid and good dude, someone I can count on no matter what.

While in barber school, I met a girl named Myra who was a complete Beatles maniac. It was at her parent's house that I watched the Beatle's first Ed Sullivan appearance. Her dad and mom sat there with us, shaking their heads as if to say, "What is this world coming to!?" When the movie "Hard Day's Night" was released, we were the first in line and she, as well as all the other girls in the theater, spent the entire movie standing in her seat, crying tears of joy and screaming her lungs out, "Oh Paul, oh Paul". That was my first lesson in the sheer power of music and celebrity, and it struck home big time.

My father bought an old beat up 12' long silver trailer and rented me a space in a trailer park on the north side of Dayton. There I lived on Red Barn Hamburgers and Cokes while I attended barber school, driving 50 miles home most weekends for a little nourishment and family love. There was a place in Dayton where all the young people hung out called Forest Park Arena, where they booked some current national and rising local talent. The house favorite was a rock and roll band called Rick & The Raiders. They were the best group in town, and I was especially drawn Rick Zehringer's guitar work and his brother, Randy's drumming.

I was there when the head of Bang Records, Bert Berns, came on stage to announce that Rick & The Raiders had just signed to Bang Records as "The McCoys" and then they played their new song, *Hang On Sloopy.*

Of course, I'm sure most people know that Rick Zehringer later changed his last name to Derringer and moved on from The McCoys to have a major career under his new name. He had a monster hit with *Rock and Roll, Hootchie Koo* and later did stints as a member of Johnny Winter's group and Edgar Winter's White Trash. His cool guitar playing can also be heard on Alice Cooper albums and occasionally in Todd Rundgren's music.

Many years later in Nashville I became friends with Paul Davis, singer and writer of such songs as *I Go Crazy* and *Ride 'em Cowboy* and he remembered that night well because he was a label-mate of the McCoys. Bang was a hot label with, *I Want Candy, Brown-Eyed Girl* by Van Morrison, and Neil Diamond's, *Solitary Man* and *Kentucky Woman.*

After graduating from barber school I spent a year working as a barber in Springfield and Lima, Ohio, then I was offered a job in Lakeview, Ohio at Ray's Barber Shop, only a block down from my buddy, Jerry's shop. I felt weird taking that job and basically becoming Jerry's competition. After waiting three long days for someone to walk through the door for a haircut, who walked in and became my first customer? My true friend, Jerry.

Finally, I got tired of sitting in my barber's chair wondering why the hell I was wasting my life waiting for another $1.50 to walk through the door. I knew there was something better waiting for me. Then, Uncle Sam wrote me a letter.

Someday I'm Gonna Rent This Town

CHAPTER 5

Boot Camp

I was 18, the Vietnam War was gaining steam and life suddenly became quite serious. The Draft Board was keen to draft us young men, and something inside of me found the thought of killing another human being quite unsettling. My father, who was a preacher and a World War II veteran, sat me down and asked me if I wanted to register as a "conscientious objector." I told him that I didn't even know what that was. With his guidance and wisdom, I decided that I should try to get into the U.S. Coast Guard. That way I could serve my country and in the process, possibly save some lives. Of course, I would have to enlist for four years instead of serving only two if I was drafted. Then again, I also wouldn't have to spend the rest of my life . . . dead. So, on a nice spring day, I hung up my barber shears, bade farewell to my family and headed to boot camp in Camp May, New Jersey . . . also known as hell.

I knew I was in trouble the moment I stepped off the bus and heard, "OK you dumb ass idiots, get your long haired, pussy butts off that bus and try to line up here like the civilian pukes you are! They used to be your mama's, but now your asses are MINE!" And that was just the *nice* things that prick had to say. I realized quickly that I was in for it and that these may not be my people.

I have little to say about boot camp other than it was a royal pain. At the end of my sentence, orders were issued and posted on the bulletin board. Imagine my joy when I saw that I was being shipped off to the Bering Sea and a five man outpost in Adak, Alaska!

I'm talking a remote frozen tundra just a few miles from Siberia! This was either a cruel joke or a bad dream. Not exactly what I was hoping for. I was hoping to be stationed in Cincinnati, on the Ohio River at a small search and rescue station, close to home. When I called and told my folks the news, there was silence on the line, then my dad said, "We'll pray about it." Well, they must have done some heavenly praying, because two days later, my orders to Adak, Alaska vanished! Instead, I had new orders to report to the U.S. Coast Guard Cutter Campbell, The Coast Guard's flagship stationed in Staten Island, New York.

To rewind a bit, when I was in boot camp I was still dating my high school sweetheart, crazy Darleen, and most nights there were the obligatory pay phone calls to Ohio. Man, boot camp can make you horny and lonely! I missed that wild stuff a lot and on one exceptionally lonely night she talked me into getting married. After leaving Cape May, en-route to my next assignment, I had two weeks leave, so I headed home to see the folks and my girlfriend. When I got back I found out that she had been screwing the local football hero while I was off guarding our coast. I had tried numerous other times to break up with Darleen, but she always went ballistic on me, one time trying to jump from my MGA going 60 miles an hour, as I held on to her belt, saving her stupid and drunken butt. Another time, in a jealous rage, she attacked me with a knife . . . but that's another story. So, I knew that there was no way to graciously exit the situation without terrible drama and paying a mighty high price. My good old dad came through for me, saying, "If you leave tonight, I will drive you to your next assignment." I never saw her nutty face again.

The Coast Guard Cutter Campbell was a 327 foot ship whose duty was to sit out in the North Atlantic for 30 days at a time, assist ships in distress, act as a checkpoint for transatlantic flights, take weather balloon readings, and track icebergs. We would sail out of Staten Island, spend a day or two in St. Johns, Newfoundland, then head out to our appointed spot called Weather Station Alpha. I reported to the ship as a lowly Seaman Apprentice, but, by a stroke of luck, ended up being the ship's barber. I knew that license would come in handy someday. So, instead of spending my time over the side of the ship painting it white with all the other newbies, I ran the ship's barber shop. Of course, the military wanted everybody's hair real short, so I was busy making plenty of extra money on the side.

Occasionally when we were back in port, I would spend all my time and pay taking the Staten Island Ferry over to Manhattan and hanging out at places like The Peppermint Lounge, home of Joey D. and The Starlighters and *The Peppermint Twist*, The Metropole, Times Square, The Cafe Wah in the Village, and many other of the hundreds of great music clubs and dives in New York City. Many a night I would head back to the ship and fall asleep on the ferry, just a little too drunk for my own good.

After five months aboard the Campbell, we got assigned the great job of escorting the annual Newport, Rhode Island to Bermuda Yacht Race. Some weekend sailors have no business whatsoever taking on the mighty Atlantic Ocean. We saved six or seven sailboats and their crews on the way down to Bermuda, then spent almost a month tied up in Bermuda's St. Georges' harbor. I spent my free time learning to snorkel the gorgeous reefs and hanging out on it's pink sand beaches. After a fast month, the party was over and we had to sail back to New York.

We left one stormy afternoon, straight through the heart of the fabled Bermuda triangle, and by midnight were motoring through some nasty high seas. Other fledgeling musicians and myself had our guitars, amps and drums, stashed up in the weather balloon shack where we would jam at every opportunity. That first night out I was down in the bowels of the ship, talking with my buddy, Blain, who ran the laundry room. I left to get us a couple of cokes, but ran into a friend who talked me into going up to the shack to jam a little. Blain got worried when I didn't return and looked all over the ship for me. They tried to call me over the ship's intercom system, but those speakers couldn't be heard over the howling wind that night up in the balloon shack, so they deduced that I had gone overboard. As we were playing some rock and roll song I felt the ship turning, but didn't really think much about it and we just kept on playing. After an hour or so, we hung it up and I went down to the main deck where all hell had broken loose . . . search lights scanning the ocean, lifeboat crews at the ready, and general mayhem. Just then, an ensign ran into me and said, "My God, it's you Stevens! You've been declared officially overboard and the captain has turned the ship around searching for you. Come on up with me to the bridge." I thought, "oh shit, I am royally screwed now." But my guardian angel was sitting on my right shoulder again because the Captain had just taken over command and was so thankful that he didn't have to report that he'd lost a crew member on his first outing. He said, "thank goodness you're safe!" Then gave me a big bear hug.

Six months on a ship is a lifetime, and the scuttlebutt was that the only way off of a ship was to get assigned to some specialty school. I looked into that and found that the only school available was Radioman school in Groton, Connecticut. So I took some tests, scored high, and made it. I was off to a fresh adventure in New England.

I don't remember much about my time by the ocean in Connecticut except that it was colder than hell up there. I found learning Morse code to be an interesting challenge and I became quite proficient at it. On weekend passes my new buddies and I would either visit the ski resorts in Vermont, club hopping in Hartford, or sometimes we even drove all the way to Boston, absolutely the coldest place I have ever been in my life! The winds off of the Atlantic Ocean cut through you like a knife.

We had the luxury of a record player in our barracks, and I played one album to death, "Changes" by Johnny Rivers. I wore out the cuts, *By The Time I Get To Phoenix, The Poor Side of Town* and *The Shadow of Your Smile*. Those are still some of my favorite songs by my favorite writers . . . such quality and so real. One night I was playing The Shadow of Your Smile and a fellow radioman came up to me and showed me a picture of his hippie wife in San Francisco, standing beautifully nude on a staircase, smoking a joint. I still can't get that picture out of my mind. I guess it was my first glimpse of the hippie lifestyle and the free love attitude that was just getting a foothold out on the west coast. Little did I know I was about to get some firsthand knowledge on that subject.

Someday I'm Gonna Rent This Town

CHAPTER 6

....

California, Here I Come!

When I was fresh out of radioman school in Groton, Connecticut, I was sent to the Coast Guard Radio Station San Francisco, on San Bruno mountain, just south of the Golden Gate Bridge, for two years.

I found myself in Golden Gate Park my first day in San Francisco, not aware that a be-in was in full swing. While gravitating to the music of the Grateful Dead playing in the distance, suddenly a beautiful blonde, suntanned California flower child, naked but for a see-through net dress, danced up, kissed me square on the mouth and handed me a joint saying, "Be groovy." I fell in love with San Francisco on the spot! I was never the same after that day. It began to dawn on me that the Coast Guard was no longer an adventure, but a prison . . . a prison I still had over three years to endure.

I was musically blessed those two years, for every weekend I would go to concerts at either the Fillmore, the Avalon Ballroom, Winterland, or on the beach at the Family Dog. These venues were the greatest and I saw the best. I heard Jimi Hendrix play a couple of times, Jefferson Airplane, the Grateful Dead, the Youngbloods, Steve Miller Band, The Sons of Champlin, It's A Beautiful Day, Big Brother and the Holding Co., The Charlatans, Muddy Waters, Howlin' Wolf, Taj Mahal, Van Morrison, Linn County, Country Joe and the Fish, Tim Hardin, Joan Baez, Arlo Guthrie, Tim Buckley, Led Zeppelin, Cream, Spencer Davis Group, Elvin Bishop, Paul Butterfield Blues Band with Mike Bloomfield, Buddy Miles, Albert King, B.B. King,

Moby Grape, H.P. Lovecraft, Spirit, Moody Blues, Emerson, Lake & Palmer, Quicksilver Messenger Service, Blue Cheer, Joe Cocker with Leon Russell, and countless others.

These concert halls didn't have assigned seating as they do nowadays. You could get right up front and stand with your elbows on the stage and head in the speakers. You haven't lived until you've seen Jimi Hendrix burn a screaming Stratocaster two feet from the tip of your nose! The Fillmore's owner was Bill Graham, and he had a quirky habit of mixing some diverse acts together in his shows. My first exposure to live country music came from seeing Area Code 615, made up of Charlie McCoy on harmonica and other Nashville session players such as Mac Gayden, Wayne Moss, Buddy Spicher, David Briggs, Norbert Putnam, Bobby Thompson, Kenny Buttrey, Ken Lauber, and Weldon Myrick, all future mainstay musicians in Nashville. They ripped it up between sets by folkies, deadheads and acid rockers.

I had two lives in California. While on duty in the United States Coast Guard I donned my uniform, sent and received Morse code, and helped make the Pacific Ocean safer for all manner of seafarers. When I was off duty though, I was becoming a full-fledged stoned hippie.

San Francisco in the mid-sixties was a magical place to be, especially when observed through a pot induced euphoria. But, to tell you the truth, the first three joints I smoked had absolutely no effect on me. I believe it was because I came from Ohio and there were multiple layers of straightness that had to be permeated. Up to that point, the only time I had even heard of marijuana was in a documentary film that they presented in our high school auditorium. In that film, these greasy-haired, turtlenecked, Greenwich village beatniks were listening to jazz, taking Hoover-sized drags off of funny-looking cigarettes, then falling down in hysterical laughter or suicidal sobbing. Oh yea, one hipster, in a raging pot high, broke off a Coke bottle and assaulted his friend with it. We all had a good laugh at that one. But, come to think of it, I did skip the senior class trip to New York City later that year.

Fresh out of Radioman School.

While living in California, I also attended the Altamont Speedway Festival. All I can say about that experience is that the film they made of the concert fails to accurately depict the terrible vibes that beset the crowd that day . . . a combination of bad drugs, worse festival conditions, Hell's Angels and dark Rolling Stones' music. As I and thousands of others stood trying to listen to the music, the Hell's Angels sat nearby on top of an old school bus, throwing full cans of beer into the audience. That made for an uptight time, trying to make sure you didn't get bashed in the head by a flying beer can. I remember one skinny hippie standing near me, buck naked, tripping on bad acid and trembling and moaning through it all. Then there was the infamous stabbing and killing of a guy up by the stage and fights breaking out here and there. The Rolling Stones kept the audience waiting for what seemed like hours, making the vibes even worse . . . all in all a miserable excuse for an outdoor concert. . . . nothing like another Woodstock at all. Rolling Stone magazine featured a photo of the crowd on the cover of it's next issue and I can identify myself standing there in my Coast Guard issued peacoat. It was the beginning of the end of the hippie movement with the last nail being driven into the coffin by non-hippie, but long haired, Charles Manson and his group of so-called love children.

Rewind:
I hung around with a bass player named Ray when I shared

an apartment with my Coast Guard buddy, Ed Chambers, in Burlingame, California. He dropped by one day to see if I wanted to go into San Francisco with him to see something "weird." That's all I needed to hear, and we were soon walking up the stairs to a third floor loft that contained an entire wall of phone jacks, hundreds of cables, electric cords, and a huge keyboard. It was a new instrument, the hippie guy running it said, called a "Moog". He sat down at the keyboard and played the strangest, unearthly electronic sounds I had ever heard since my uncle Bob's theremin. Looking back on that day, I realize that I saw one of the very first synthesizers, the forerunner of instruments I've used a thousand times in the recording studio ever since.

Being a hippie at heart and Coast Guardsman by trade was not an easy coexistence. There was so much about the military that was anti-individual. Sometimes I entertained serious thoughts of bailing out and getting lost in the subculture I was precariously living in. I suppose the fact that I had some real close friends in the same boat pulled me through and allowed me to stick it out. Of course I'm proud of some of the things I accomplished in the Coast Guard. I figure I was instrumental in saving at least eight or nine lives during my tour of duty. That part of my service was rewarding and interesting, but the rest just rubbed me the wrong way, especially when it came to some of the lifers that barked the orders. Unfortunately these are the ones who can rise in rank, apparently for no reason other than their length of service.

A case in point: later, while stationed as radioman in charge at Monterey Lifeboat Station, I encountered a Boatswain's Mate 1st Class that didn't get along with me, or anyone else for that matter . . . a real gung-ho ass. I think he got word that I was hanging out with hippie-dippy types and attending protest rallies and singing "subversive" songs in folk clubs during my off time. One night while manning the radios, I got a distress call that a commercial fisherman had found a "floater," or dead body, in Monterey Bay. Normally the Boatswain's Mate would round up a couple of seamen for this pickup mission, but due to a shortage of personnel on base that night, he arranged for me to go. When we finally found the body, it was terribly apparent that it had been swimming with the fishes for much too long. To add to the disgusting nature of the situation, large shrimp had attached themselves all over the poor guy's body. After bringing him into the boat, we headed back to the base. Much to my horror, the Boatswain's Mate began picking the shrimp off of the corpse and depositing them in a bucket he had brought along. In disbelief I asked, "what the hell are you doing?" He said, "Oh just taking home some free supper for the family." I about puked.

After two years in San Francisco, I was transferred to the lifeboat station in Monterey. I lived off base in a small cabin in Carmel and began oil painting in much of my free time, selling my works at a Fisherman's Wharf gallery located in an old converted fish cannery. This was the place John Steinbeck wrote about in his book "Cannery Row," long before it turned into a tourist attraction and the Aquarium was built. I spent all off time I could on my motorcycle, running' down beautiful Highway One, the coast road through Big Sur . . . no prettier place on earth. There was this one secluded beach I found there that I went to often. I was walking down it one foggy morning, when I thought I saw three large dogs running towards me. When they got closer I realized that they were actually large wild boars. I had to make a hasty retreat into the freezing surf as they ran by. Later I found out that beach was the one where they shot the film, "The Sandpipers" starring Elizabeth Taylor and Richard Burton.

It was on those all night radio watches at Monterey station that I began writing poetry. I amassed quite a bit of material in the year and a half spent there, and some of those ideas ended up in some of my songs many years later. It was there that I started writing songs to play in local folk clubs. Rather than perform only other artist's tunes, I began throwing in a few of my own originals and found that they went over well. I began thinking of myself as a "songwriter." I had vague dreams of having other artists record my compositions, but I hadn't a clue how to make that dream come true.

One day I received a phone call from John, a hippie who I had hung out with in San Francisco. He was now a road manager and had an upcoming gig with a Detroit hard rock group named Catfish. They were about to make a two week long run of the west coast, playing places like the Fillmore West, Avalon Ballroom, and the Whiskey A-Go-Go and he asked if I'd like to take a job as a roadie. I had some leave time coming, so I took it and met up with John and the band in San Francisco. Now this was one kick-ass rowdy band, made up of ex-members of the old Mitch Ryder & the Detroit Wheels and the heavy metal band, MC5. I was a real lightweight compared to these guys when it came to getting high! They would do any drug, in any quantity, in any combination, at any moment of the day or night, (except for the lead singer, Bob Hodge, who I think stayed straight). They loved nothing more than doing four or five different magic potions, then hit the stage for a performance. I don't know how they maintained this, but they were great and they *Rocked*! Unfortunately, being as stoned as they always were, they weren't the world's best business men. They were always broke and asking me to call management in Detroit for more advances. It got to the point where management just got fed up. The band was third on the bill at the Fillmore behind Rod Stewart and the Small Faces, and electronic rocker, Lee Michaels. Backstage was a three-ring circus, with copious amounts of booze, drugs, and groupies. All the members of Catfish had women hanging on them and they were waiting for me to show up with their individual advances from Detroit so that they could afford to party on into the night. When I did arrive, they asked for their money, but I tried to convince them to let me give it to them in private, for I knew it was going to be a major embarrassment. They kept insisting, so I handed them what the fed-up management had sent . . . *Ten dollars each*! I never saw groupies leave rock stars so fast in my life.

One night, in an L.A. hotel, the subject came up that I wrote songs, and the guys in the band wanted to hear some of them. Lo and behold they thought they were pretty good! The lead guitar player said, "Shit man, that song's as good as anything out there on the radio." Looking back, I guess I owe a lot to that guy. His words stoked my creative fire and gave me more inspiration to pursue a song writing career.

Someday I'm Gonna Rent This Town

CHAPTER 7

North to Alaska

On a sunny day in February 1970 my tour of duty with the U.S. Coast Guard was up. I had a ritual "all-things-Coast Guard" burning on a Carmel beach, packed up my guitar and headed for Alaska. Ed Chambers, a west coast friend with whom I worked at San Francisco Radio Station, had three months until his discharge from his Ketchikan station. He had a remote cabin with no electricity or running water right on the ocean, about twelve miles from town, that I called home for a while. I flew from Seattle into the wilderness on a seaplane and discovered that Ketchikan, Alaska was a real frontier town with wooden sidewalks, beaver pelt stores and Eskimo totem poles. I felt like a hippie John Wayne up there. There weren't many distractions other than the bar in town, so I spent my time getting stoned, writing songs, and hiking around the forests and magnificent coastline. When Ed had a few weeks to go, I bummed a ride with another west coaster down to Prince Rupert Island, where we caught a ferry, then drove through some Canadian snowstorms, Washington state and Oregon, down the coast highway until we reached California. When Ed got discharged we met up and relocated to his parents house in El Cajon, near San Diego. I stayed in their pool house for a month or so, smoked a lot of weed, sat in at a few clubs, then decided it was time to head back home to Ohio to regroup.

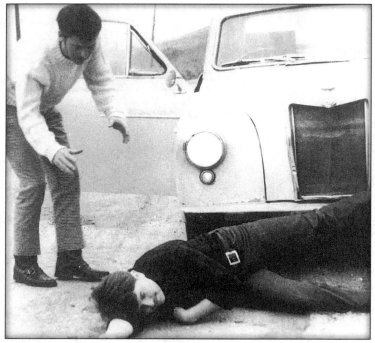

My first film roll (35mm) with El Cajon star Ed Chambers in "The Accident".

CHAPTER 8

....

Nashville Calling

I had quite a few songs, but no idea what to do with them, so I began thinking of alternatives. I applied to the Dayton Art Institute with the intention of becoming a graphic artist, when out of the blue, I got a call from my uncle Bob, who I hadn't seen in years. He was living in Nashville trying to get a foothold in session work as a drummer and recording engineer. At the time he was playing in the house band at a club on lower Broadway called the Demon's Den, owned by country star Web Pierce. Bob had heard that I was writing songs and invited me to come down, and offered to introduce me to the few singers he knew who might be interested in recording them. I was broke and my family was out of town, so I borrowed forty bucks from our next door neighbor, loaded up my old International Scout mail truck, with the steering wheel on the right side, and made my pilgrimage to Music City, USA.

Nashville, Tennessee couldn't have been more foreign to me if it had been Bumfuck, Egypt. I expected to see hitching posts in front of all the buildings. After all, I was coming from Ohio, by way of California and Alaska, and didn't have a clue what to expect. My hair was real long, and that in itself made me an outsider. After all, these were the days when even Willie Nelson and Waylon Jennings still had those slick Brylcreem haircuts.

I arrived late that night and went directly to the club to watch my uncle play country cover tunes until the 2 am closing time. While they were tearing down their equipment, I noticed an old acoustic guitar leaning by the restroom door and began playing one of my songs, called *Fair Weather Friends*. As luck would have it, Web Pierce himself walked by, stopped to listen and said, "You know what? That song right there would be perfect for my daughter Debbie to record. Would you like to have it published?" Well, I said, "You bet!" and we went to his publishing company, he called in his secretary at two in the morning, I sang my song into a tape recorder, signed a publishing contract, and the rest was history! The next day I called all my songwriting friends in California and said, "Come on down to Nashville, this is *EASY!*"

I crashed in my uncle's attic, and every few weeks I would go to Web's office and ask the receptionist when Debbie would be recording my song. She assured me that, "Debbie loves your song, and will be cutting it any day now." Well, this went on for six months or so, until I finally got fed up with the whole deal and demanded my song back if Debbie wasn't going to record it. The receptionist looked at me sheepishly and replied, "I've got a confession to make . . . I'm Debbie, I lost your tape right after I got it, and I was too embarrassed to say anything." It was three long years before I ever got one of my songs recorded.

Although *Fair Weather Friends* never saw the light of the recording studio, that slim promise of success kept me in Nashville, blowing off the idea of Art School and letting me absorb the culture that was Music City in those exciting times. Kris Kristofferson was already familiar to me from album cuts on records that I bought in California. It didn't really dawn on me that his songs were "country" at the time, I just knew that I liked them in the same way that I liked Bob Dylan's "Nashville Skyline" album or Creedence Clearwater Revival. Hard country was not my cup-of-tea, but I thought that I could make it as a songwriter in the vein of Kris's work or, another favorite, Mickey Newbury. Mickey was a champion for a couple of new writers, Guy Clark and Townes Van Zandt, and somewhere along the line my first year in town, I met Guy Clark. He surprised me one day and took me out to Mickey's house on Old Hickory Lake to meet him. That house was like walking into a songwriter's secret hideaway, with beautiful guitars sitting all around . . . I could just imagine those moody songs of his being created in that living room. Very magic indeed, and I've always appreciated Guy Clark for that generous gesture and gift to an unknown fellow songwriter.

To my great luck, I fell into the songwriting crowd with similar tastes as mine. Writers like Chris Gantry, *Dreams of the Everyday Housewife*, Lee Clayton, *Ladies Love Outlaws*, Vince Matthews, *Love In The Hot Afternoon*, Peck Chandler, Jim Casey, Buzz Rabin and many others of the same ilk. I played my early songs for Johnny McRae at Kristofferson's publishing home, Combine Music. He didn't sign me, but in the process I met a young fellow named Johnny Johnson, who was in charge of the four track recording studio, and he allowed me to come in and use the studio to get my songs down in the middle of the nights when it wasn't being used by their staff songwriters. It was great recording in the little studio where, I was told, Bobbie Gentry laid down the basic guitar & vocal of Ode to Billy Joe.

My uncle's contacts didn't pan out too well, but I knocked on door after door and made call after call trying to see whomever I could who would give me an appointment. This was before cassettes were the standard and all my songs were on reel-to-reel tapes and that's how I pitched my songs. I remember one meeting with a producer named Dick Heard. He put my tape on his machine and as it played he held his thumb against the reel to slow it down because his machine was running too fast. I sat there in amazement as my voice went from sounding like Alvin the Chipmunk to Tennessee Ernie Ford as he tried to make it play the right speed. He reviewed and rejected two of my songs with this method and then I snapped! "You gotta be kidding me" I said, walked over, rewound my tape and stormed out of his office thinking, "What an asshole." Amazingly, he ended up cutting many of my songs later and we became friends.

Rejection is a way of life for an aspiring song writer in Nashville, Tennessee. You develop a thick skin as your career progresses.

If you don't, it'll drive you crazy. Luckily I met a few good Samaritans along the way. Judy Thomas at Tree International, publisher of songs by Willie Nelson, Merle Haggard, Buck Owens, Jim Reeves, and Roger Miller, was one of my early believers. She would publish some songs and arrange for some small advances for me with the owners, Buddy Killen and Jack Stapp, and that would keep me alive for a month or two. Money was scarce, but I had real low overhead. I slept in my Scout most nights and relied on the kindness of strangers when it got too cold outside. Another publisher who helped me was Chuck Glaser of the famous Glaser Brothers. Besides having hits as artists themselves, Chuck, Jim, and Tompall had just had a big publishing success with *Gentle On My Mind*, written by John Hartford, and were open to more progressive-type songs. Chuck took me into their studio and let me record my demos with some top-of-the-line players. It was there that I first met recording engineer Kyle Lehning, who would let me come and sit in discreetly in the back of the room and watch as famous, and not so famous people, recorded their records. Kyle later became hugely successful producing England Dan & John Ford Coley, one of the earliest pop acts to make it big out of Nashville, as well as Randy Travis, Kenny Rogers, Ronnie Milsap and many others.

Chuck's office was always an interesting place to be. The beginnings of the outlaw movement in Nashville was forming and Tompall Glaser and his cohorts were in the forefront of it. All the songwriters with something a little more edgy to say hung out there and at Marie Barrett's house right next door. I met Johnny Darrell, John Hartford, Peck Chandler, Buzz Rabin, and others there and started to get a more focused idea of what kind of songs I wanted to write. Marie's was a wonderful place. She was a lover of country music and those who wrote it. It didn't matter to her if you were famous or not, her home was open to whoever wanted to fall by, and some days she was the only reason I had anything to eat. There were a many "guitar pulls," the original In The Round, on her living room floor, when a group of writers would take turns passing the guitar, showing each other their newest creations. I'll always be grateful to Marie for befriending me and encouraging me that I had the kind of songs that would someday be recorded. In later years Marie handled Shel Silverstein's publishing company and married the late, great John Hartford.

It was at the Glaser Brothers' where I started hanging out with songwriter Buzz Rabin. He had just had his song *Beaucoups of Blues* chosen to be the title song on Ringo Starr's country album, produced by steel guitar wizard, Pete Drake, recorded after the Beatles breakup. Buzz and I teamed up for a short time and once decided to hit the road together for a gig in Kansas City. We made it thirty miles shy of KC when my Scout ran out of gas and we ran out of money. We flagged down an ancient black gentleman in a rusted old flatbed truck and he kindly pushed us up the highway to the nearest gas station. Buzz sold him his pocket knife and six Ringo Starr albums, one for each of his kids, and we made it in time for our big debut at the Oak Hotel in Kansas City. When we checked in we discovered that it was a real hole. Our room had a bare bulb hanging from a wire in the ceiling and the bedspread and curtains were stained and the rug was filthy and thread bare. The situation got worse when I went down to the lounge to play my songs for a suspiciously all male audience. After the fourth guy sent drinks and winked at me on stage, I took an early break and went upstairs to let Buzz in on the news. The booking agent hadn't told us we were going to Kansas City to play a gay bar. Buzz just calmly stood there in his underwear, pressing his pants, smiled and reminded me that we had been paid up front. So, while I loaded up the gear, he took a magic marker and wrote across the wall in big, huge letters, " BUZZ AND EVEN TRIED HERE, BUT BUZZ AND EVEN DIED HERE, BESIDES, THEY'RE ALL QUEER HERE!!!!"

Back in Nashville I continued to play my songs whenever and wherever I could at open mic nights, and at places like the Exit Inn, Bishops Pub, and The Red Dog Saloon. I'd pass the hat and live from day to day on the few bucks I took in. Peggy Hanson, a female friend of mine, took over the Red Dog Saloon and changed it's name to Calamity Jane's and let me move into the attic. It was while living there that Charlie Daniels and his band rented a tiny room and spent every day jamming and rehearsing. I knew who Charlie was from the credits on one of my favorite albums, Bob Dylan's "Nashville Skyline," so I snuck in every chance I could to listen to the fine playing going on. Little did I know that I was witnessing history in the making in that little room. Soon they recorded *Uneasy Rider* and they were off and running.

During the time I stayed there I met some very talented people, like the soulful singer Tracy Nelson, and manager, Travis Rivers of "Mother Earth" fame, Billy Swan, *I Can Help* and Kinky Friedman, *Get Your Biscuits In the Oven and Your Buns In the Bed*. They were next door neighbors. I lived there for nearly six months, until the summer came and that attic temperature rose to a hellacious 115 degrees, so I moved back into my wheels and wondered why I wasn't a hit song writer yet.

Meanwhile, uncle Bob got an offer to go to Martin, Tennessee, a little town near Memphis, to build and operate a recording studio in a defunct airport hanger for a record producer from Detroit by the name of Otis Ellis. Bob asked me if I wanted to make some dough helping him wire the studio and I figured, why not, things weren't exactly on fire for me in Nashville. The night before we were to leave, Bob had a terrible accident and cut some of the tendons in his arm. That left me to do the physical building and Bob to do the advising. It took us about three months to get the studio up and running, and as a bonus, Otis took a liking to my singing and offered me the chance to record an album of my songs. During the process I began to notice that Otis was remixing old tapes he had brought down from Detroit and releasing them as early Grand Funk Railroad records. Actually they were outtakes by Terry Knight and the Pack, with future Grand Funk member, Mark Farner, on bass guitar. Now, something about this didn't sit right with me, so I made my exit from the situation before I signed any contracts and got in too deep. My album project was adequate, not terrific, but I got valuable studio experience as an artist and as a studio builder, which came in handy years later.

Eventually I got the urge to be back in Music City where the songwriting action was. Much to my surprise, I got a coveted appointment with the principals at the most happening publishing company in Nashville, owned by some producers who were making the hippest and out-of-the-box music in town. Located on the top of a famous studio, Quadraphonic Sound, the place to record, I sat nervously waiting for them to hear my songs. They were underwhelmed! They told me I should move back to Ohio and find another line of work.

Fast forward twenty years: I ran into the legendary producer and publisher Norbert Putnam, who rejected my songs that day, and he told me, "You know Even, I've made two judgement calls in my career that I regret to this day. Number one: Kenny Rogers came to me with a song called, *Lucille*, stating that, "This is the song I am going to make my big comeback with in music." I told him in so many words, 'Don't call me, I'll call you.' Mistake number two: Telling you to give up song writing. I passed up a gold mine."

My songs in those early days were folk and rock based, and not what was happening in mainstream country at the time, although there were unique records being made in Nashville, such as *Please Come To Boston* by Dave Loggins and *The Night They Drove Old Dixie Down* by Joan Baez, but they were not the norm.

Another appointment that I got after many tries was at April-Blackwood Publishing. The man in charge there didn't particularly like my tunes, but saw promise. He reached into his desk and handed me a Billy Joel songbook and told me to study it. I didn't really like the songs of Billy Joel at the time, and I told him that I didn't want to write like Billy Joel . . . I wanted to write like Even Stevens, and left again, disappointed and dejected. Some would probably say that was an ego move but I had great faith that I was on the right track and had something new to offer country music. I thought, "time will tell."

CHAPTER 9

. . . .

Eddie Rabbitt

One night I was invited to a party and there I met Eddie Rabbitt. He asked me if I would help him move to a new apartment the next day and I said I would. Turns out, he had a pet monkey he kept in a large cage in his apartment and asked if we could transport the cage in my jeep. It was pretty damn funky, so I said, "hell no dude . . . I don't know you *that* well, and besides, I sleep in there!" We tied it on top of my jeep instead and that was the beginning of our lifelong friendship. We played our songs for each other at first, but didn't try to write songs together for a long time, mainly because we were into totally different musical styles. Eddie was writing hard core country while I was more folk and rock oriented.

About this time I wrangled an appointment with Ray Stevens. His studio manager, Ann, had taken a real interest in my songs. The truth be known, secretaries basically run the Nashville music business. If you don't hit it off with them, you might as well hang it up getting to see their bosses. Ann persuaded Ray to see me.

I was very nervous meeting Ray Stevens. I'd been a big fan and bought his quirky stuff like *Ahab The Arab* and *Guitarzan* when I was a teenager in Ohio, so I was meeting a real star. He couldn't have been nicer to me and we struck up a working relationship. He was in the final stages of building a beautiful new recording studio he called Ray Steven's Sound Lab and I was the first to record there. Ray let me book any musicians I wanted for my first Nashville session, so I hired all my friends and all their friends. I had John Hartford on fiddle, acoustic guitar whiz Norman Blake, Kyle Tuttle on electric bass, Karl Himmel on drums, with Ben Talent as engineer. All in all, seven or eight players were hired and I told them to "play whatever they wanted to play," the kiss of death for any session. I thought it went great and I had a ball, but when Ray and I listened to it the next day we just laughed and threw up our hands. It was a real traffic jam of sound, and somewhere in there was my voice, trying it's best to be heard. That session did lead to more sane recordings and I enjoyed working with Ray Stevens tremendously, but he was consumed with writing and recording his own records and confessed that he didn't really have the time to lend to my artistic aspirations. He did offer me a deal to write for his publishing company, but I decided to hold off and try to find someone who was interested in me on both fronts, as a songwriter and recording artist.

Rewind:

One great gift that came out of meeting Ray Stevens was the friendship that developed between his staff songwriter, Layng Martine Jr., and myself. What a jewel of a person Layng was and is. A unique songwriter, with classic songs like Billy "Crash" Craddock's *Rub It In* and Elvis's last hit, *Way Down* . . . and the fabulous song that Reba made popular *The Greatest Man I Never Knew,* co-written with the great Richard Leigh. Layng and I used to stand outside of Ray Stevens Sound Lab and try to figure out how to raise money to make Eddie Rabbitt a star, long before it happened for him. A special friend indeed.

A few weeks later I was walking down the street when a young fellow in a Porsche pulled up beside me and asked if I was Even Stevens. Thinking he might be a bill collector, I asked him why he wanted to know and he said, "My father is Jim Malloy, and he's interested in meeting with you about your songs." Turns out this kid was David Malloy who was fresh out of high school and an assistant engineer at the Sound Lab, whom I had never met. Ray's secretary had told him about me and my writing. I had certainly heard of Jim

Malloy. He had recently produced the CMA Song of the Year, *Help Me Make It Through The Night*, a Grammy winner written by Kris Kristofferson and recorded by Sammi Smith, and it was one of my favorite songs by one of my favorite singers. I was totally excited that Jim Malloy wanted to meet me. Jim was not only a major record producer, but was legendary in the world of sound engineering, working in Los Angeles and in Nashville on records by a long list of greats, such as Frank Sinatra, Dean Martin, Sam Cooke, Timi Yuro, Al Hirt, Elvis Presley, Roy Orbison, Hank Jr., Ike and Tina Turner, Willie Nelson, Waylon Jennings, Dolly Parton, George Jones, Jerry Lee Lewis, Charley Pride, Henry Mancini, Duane Eddy, Neil Diamond, Linda Ronstadt, Eddy Arnold, Doris Day, Mahalia Jackson, Ray Stevens, Bing Crosby, Sammy Davis, Jr., Paul Anka, Ricky Nelson, The Carter Family, The Stoneman Family, Jack Benny, Perry Como, Anita Kerr Singers, Bobby Gentry, Lefty Frizzell, Lightnin' Hopkins, Jack Clement, Tennessee Ernie Ford and The Beach Boys . . . Jim was even recording with Sam Cooke the very day he was shot and killed. He also won engineering Grammys for his work with Henry Mancini and was in charge of the sound for the groundbreaking Johnny Cash Show. He engineered classic records for David Seville's, The Chipmunks . . . and he wanted to meet me! Gulp!

That meeting was a turning point in my song writing career. Jim liked my songs and offered me a publishing deal on the spot and promised that he'd do all he could to get me an artist's deal, with himself as producer as well. He set up a new publishing company for my compositions and named it DebDave Music, after his children's first names, Debbie and David, and I was assured that if things went well, in few years I would be made half owner of the company. Jim took me under his wing and fed me, fronted me money to live on, bought me a car, entertained me, and introduced me to everyone he knew, always letting them know that he thought I was the greatest. He gave me tons of much needed encouragement and I responded with a fury of songwriting. Jim Malloy will always own a special place in my heart.

My first cut was a song I wrote by myself. I was thrilled that my favorite singer, Sammi Smith, recorded *I'm In For Stormy Weather*, on her album, "The Toast of '45." Turns out, that record gave me my first lesson in humility.

Bob Montgomery, Buddy Holly's ex-singing partner and successful record producer and publisher, had a party at his barn-turned-into-a-house in the country, and for some unknown reason, I was invited. In the living room there was a record player and a stack of albums, and to my pleasant surprise, Sammi's new album was there. I covertly arranged for the album to make it onto the turntable next and struck up a conversation with a pretty young thing, hoping to impress her with my song writing prowess. I finagled the topic of discussion towards the selections on Sammi Smith's new album, and discovered that the girl was a rabid fan of Sammi's and her music. Just then my song began to play. It was a beautiful moment, and then the girl said, "I love Sammi Smith, but why she ever chose to record that piece of shit, I'll never know."

Soon Eddie Rabbitt and I began writing songs together and we hit on something special, something totally different than we wrote on our own. It flowed like a river, sometimes we wrote two or three songs a day. Then, in 1974, Eddie and I pitched a crazy song to producer Ray Pennington at RCA called *Que Pasa* and he recorded it on the rotund, Kenny Price, of Hee Haw fame. It went top thirty on the charts. Kenny had just come off a big hit, *The Sheriff of Boone County*, where he, as the redneck sheriff said, "you're in a heap o' trouble boy." Now he was on the radio singing our song with the lyrics, "Let's go loco on my Acapulco." We were amazed. We presented Kenny with a super huge sombrero that he wore on stage when he preformed our song on the Grand Ole Opry. One day in Ray's office Kenny asked us what the "Acapulco line" in the song meant, and we didn't have the heart to tell the Sheriff of Boone County that he was singing about the pleasures of getting high on very primo pot.

I had another of my many rude awakenings during that period of my songwriting career. I was sitting in a bar at the TGIF restaurant, Thank God It's Friday, when this red head beauty of a girl walked in and sat down on the stool next to me. It was super loud in there, and we began talking and got along well. She told me her name, and I told her mine was Even Stevens. I saw the light bulb come on over her head as she said, "I've heard of you!" and I naturally thought, "of course you have, I've got a song by Kenny Price that's number 69 on the Billboard Charts!" We ended up back at her place. One thing led to another, and soon we were lying in the sweet afterglow of lust. She turned to me and said, "you know, I *really* love your music." I humbly offered my heartfelt thanks, and then she continued, "especially the song, *Everything Is Beautiful.*" A heat wave rush came over me as I realized that she thought she had just gone to bed with RAY Stevens, not EVEN Stevens! When I regained my composure I owned up that I wasn't Ray, but that I *knew* him, if that helped in any way. She took it very well and we had a good laugh about it, but I just had to go in the bathroom, look in the mirror and say, "there you go again, letting your ego run amuck!"

Someday I'm Gonna Rent This Town

CHAPTER 10

....

Ralph Emery & WSM Radio

Perhaps the most famous country radio personality in the world, Ralph Emery, took a liking to Eddie and myself and gave us great encouragement. Quite often Eddie and I would write a new song and call Ralph to tell him about it in the middle of his all-night radio broadcast on WSM. He would say, "well come on up to the hill and I'll play it on the show." We'd show up at two in the morning and darned if he wouldn't interview us and play our new creation for the whole world to hear. When Ralph began his television show on TNN he would often have Eddie and I on and would generously give myself and new artists that I produced, spots on his show. Those were the days in Nashville, loose and free. People were actually happy for your success and eager to help you in any way they could. Such a person was Ralph Emery, and he'll always be a hero to me.

Someday I'm Gonna Rent This Town

CHAPTER 11

....

The Nashville Drug Scene

Kenny Price's innocence about marijuana was typical of how things were in Nashville in the early 70's. I'm sure everyone has heard about the huge amount of speed that was being consumed by Johnny Cash at that time. I once went with a songwriter friend to a doctor's office on the East side of the Cumberland River. When we walked into the waiting room, both sides of the room were lined up with Nashville's best song writers, musicians and artists, waiting to get in to see the doctor for a prescription for "chronic fatigue." The doc would write you out a "scrip" for Pancakes, White Crosses, Speckled Birds, L.A. Turnarounds . . . (you took one, drove to L.A., turned around and drove back), Yellows, or whatever your fancy. You paid your thirty bucks and you were off on your speedy way. If you check out some of the big hits of that era, you'll find they had more lyrical alliteration than a rap song. Writers would stay up for four or five days at a stretch. It was called "being on a roar." Everybody hung out at the Country Corner, located where Curb Records now stands on Music Row, or Linebaugh's restaurant, downtown on Broadway, doing uppers and thinking lots of fast thoughts.

Long-haired guys like me were few-and-far-between and not always greeted with the best of attitudes. After all, this was the home of Country Music. Songs like *Okee From Muskogee, The Fightin' Side of Me,* and *Ballad of the Green Berets* were very popular, and it was common knowledge that Country and Hippie just didn't mix. One shaggy acquaintance of mine was a writer named Townes Van Zandt.

Now Townes was a very dark human being. He used to show up at my basement apartment around seven in the morning, en route to a 10 a.m. demo session with his guitar in one hand and a fifth of booze in the other and proceed to get righteously smashed. One morning Townes and I decided we would go get something to eat at the Pancake Pantry, a popular breakfast place on the edge of Music Row. The old fellow who owned the place at the time didn't like longhairs and refused to let us in. I was getting used to that sort of thing, but Townes didn't take it so well. He told me the next day that he went back that night when they were closed and threw a brick through their window. One of the rare times I ever saw Townes really happy.

CHAPTER 12

....

Music Row Characters

Nashville, and especially the Music Row area, had no shortage of eccentric characters. Some that come to mind were, Zilch Fletcher, Arizona Star & George, Captain Midnight, Travis Rivers, Chris Gantry, Paul Craft, Jim Rooney, Marshal Chapman, Pebble Daniel, Sandy Mason, Peck Chandler, Kim Morrison and David Allen Coe. But, the cherry on top of the fruitcake was, Cowboy Jack Clement, famous for saying, "if you're not having fun, you're not doing your job!" My sentiments exactly.

I met Jack for the first time hanging with Jim Malloy. Another friend of mine, Spady Brannon, who later became a staff writer for our company, used to have a unique job with Cowboy Jack. Jack liked to stroll around his house with guitar in hand and play music all day. He devised a portable sound system, consisting of a tiny lavalier microphone that he taped to the bridge of his nose, ran the chord over his head and down through his shirt, and plugged in to a small pig nose amplifier, powered by batteries hanging on his belt. Spady would follow him around the The Cowboy Arms Hotel and Recording Spa playing bass guitar with it plugged in to his own personal amp on his belt. It sounded damn good and was a humorous sight to see. Spady made a weekly salary doing this and keeping joints rolled and on hand for Cowboy Jack. They were like a two-man traveling show.

On one occasion, my friend Jim was sitting across from Jack at his desk. There was an open window on the wall between them and a small bird landed there and within a few seconds a cat appeared from nowhere and pounced on the bird, killed and ate it right in front of them. There was a moment of silence, then Jack said, "it's a jungle out there Jim."

I used to love to go to a Music Row club called Spats back in the 1970's, only because occasionally Cowboy would put on a music revue-type show starring a cavalcade of local talent, including, two identically dressed soul singers named Rick Shulman, a big strapping fellow with great pipes, and Little Ricky Jarvis, a dwarf, also with great pipes. They would come out and rock the stage, dancing and singing to Sam and Dave songs. There was telling who Jack would have on the show, but they were diverse and always great. He had Nashville's finest musicians on stage with a horn section featuring Dennis Solee, a conga player and who knows what else. Eventually Jack would samba out to the music of Brazil, with a full shot glass of whiskey balanced on top of his head, never spilling a drop, then break into song. That show was always so nuts and crazy . . . Jack Clement was born to be on stage.

My mentor and friend, Jim Malloy recorded the definitive Jack Clement album . . . the one with Jack on the cover swinging on a swing. It's called "All I Want To Do In Life" and contains fine renditions of *When I Dream, Good Hearted Woman* and *It'll Be Her*. I had the privilege to hang around during some of the recordings and it was quite an experience. Jack would record version after version, take after take of a song, filling up 24 track tape like it was nothing, bent on getting just the right feel. He was the master of feel and that album is a classic for sure.

Another pair of Music Row characters were songwriters Vince Matthews and Jim Casey. Vince was an intense sort who never seemed to run out of energy, be it natural or chemically induced. He and Jim Casey were inseparable buddies. You never saw one without the other. They wrote tons of songs together. Perhaps Vince's biggest claim to fame was writing, *On Susan's Floor*, a soulful song, co-written with Shel Silverstein, that Johnny Cash recorded all about vagabond songwriters and a woman who loved them. Vince and Kent Westbury also scored big with Gene Watson's version of *Love In The Hot Afternoon*. Jim Casey and Vince also wrote and preformed *The Kingston Springs Suite*, a slew of songs about the everyday life of the people of their small town, with the production and recording help of Shel Silverstein, Jack Clement, Johnny Cash and Kris Kristofferson.

Vince's wife Melba was a beautiful sweetheart of a woman and smart as a whip. They had this great little bungalow of a house in Kingston Springs, Tennessee, about twenty miles out of Nashville. On my first visit there one cold winter night, she insisted that I stay over instead of sleeping in my International Scout on the streets of Music Row. She and Vince gave up their big overstuffed feather bed for me to sleep in. It was like paradise and I was so grateful for a bit of relief from the street life.

One 4th of July, they had a big celebration in the town square of Kingston Springs and Vince and Jim invited me to come play some of my songs during the festivities. They had a hay wagon set up for a stage and we had a ball doing our songs. After I played, some old codger invited me to partake of some moonshine he had just made. This was my first moonshine adventure, though I don't remember that much about it. They tell me I clogged with Tracy Nelson and everyone else in town for hours, and I'd never clogged before in my life! I woke up the next morning in the back of my Scout parked in front of Eddie Rabbitt's apartment on Belmont Avenue in Nashville. My guardian angel must have been working overtime on that drive that night.

On another occasion, Vince asked me if I wanted to go to Johnny Cash's birthday party at The House of Cash recording studio out in Hendersonville. "Heck," I said, "of course I do!" We were hanging there with studio musicians, neighbors and family members when Johnny came into the room. I've never experienced such charisma before. He certainly appeared larger than life, and what amazed me the most was when he opened up a present of a pair of black socks, he was so gracious and appreciative! I couldn't believe Johnny Cash was so happy to receive black socks for his birthday! Just one of those cool memories that will always stick in my mind.

CHAPTER 13

....

Off and Running

In 1972, Eddie moved into one side of a duplex off of Bowling Avenue and when the other side of the house became available I rented it, and we got down to some serious collaborating. We even installed an intercom between our two places so we could discuss ideas whenever they struck. We wrote songs day and night and demoed them on our sound-on-sound quarter inch tape recorders, figuring out a way to bounce the tracks back and forth, first laying down a guitar and vocal, then bouncing that over to the other side while beating on the strings of a guitar for a snare drum sound and adding a harmony vocal at the same time. Then bouncing all of that back to the original track and adding the sound of a cupped hand on the back of the guitar for a bass drum and another harmony, and bouncing it one last time, for the final overdub which was usually the bass guitar, played on the top two strings of an electric Fender guitar. Our demos got a reputation around town for being really different and having a unique sound to them. With their slapback effects, they were the forerunner to the rockabilly sound we used later in the studio for some of our biggest hits like, *Drivin' My Life Away* and *B-B-B-Burnin' Up With Love*.

We started getting quite a few of our songs recorded by artists like Stonewall Jackson, Billy Walker, Mel Street, and Johnny Bush. In fact, Johnny Bush recorded the first version of *Drinkin' My Baby Off of My Mind*.

One of my solo written songs, *Put 'em All Together (I'd Have*

You), recorded by George Jones, became a top twenty hit. What a feather in my songwriting cap that was! George Jones the Legend! The artist with the most radio hits of anyone in the world . . . ever! I was starting to feel like a real professional.

CHAPTER 14

....

Sammi Smith

When God made Sammi, as they say, He broke the mold. What a character, and what a voice. I wrote a song for her with Jim Malloy titled *The Days That End in Y* that made the top thirty. Her voice was so sultry, real, and understated. We even recorded a duet together for Elektra Records called *Huckelberry Pie*, a song that I wrote based on a poem my grandfather used to recite to me when I was a child. It was nonsensical and offbeat, but it did chart and we had a great time singing it on stage. Sammi kept on blessing me with recordings on most of her albums, and I spent one year as her opening act on the road.

One gig we played was at a Christian college in Lubbock, Texas. The reason we were booked there at all was on the strength of Sammi's Grammy success with the Kristofferson song *Help Me Make It Through The Night*. Just before we were to go on stage, the president of the college came into the dressing room and asked Sammi not to sing that song. He said the lyrics were too suggestive for his students. Sammi looked at me with a devilish smile on her face and then said to the president of the Christian college, "Oh that's OK, I'm getting tired of singing that frickin' song anyway!" but she didn't use the word frickin'.

During that show, she kept whispering to me, "there's an Indian medicine man in the audience." She was kind of psychic that way, spending much of her youth growing up on an Indian reservation. Sure enough, after the show he came backstage and introduced himself. By the way, true to form, she sang *Help Me Make It Through The Night* that evening anyhow!

There were many nights during our shows that Sammi would come lean on my shoulder and say, "I'm about to pass out." I'd signal backstage and lead her over to the wings into someone's arms just before she collapsed. We covered it well, and I don't think many audiences were aware of what was going on. When we got off the road Sammi would see some doctors, but they couldn't figure out what was causing this malady. In the years towards the end of her life we stayed in touch and she was battling Lupus. Maybe that was the source of her troubles all along. I doubt if many people are aware that Waylon Payne, the actor who portrayed Jerry Lee Lewis in the Johnny Cash biography picture, "Walk The Line", is Sammi Smith's son.

Someday I hope the music world will truly realize what an incredible artist Sammi Smith was. My favorite recording she ever made was of a song called *Saunders Ferry Lane*, a song written by Delores Whitehead & Janette Tooley. If you want a treat, check it out. Sammi was the country Dusty Springfield to my mind. I'm proud to say she recorded many on my songs and was my great friend.

Rewind:

One night while Sammi and I were on tour, we were booked at a colosseum in Charlotte, North Carolina with wild man, Jerry Lee Lewis on the bill. At an early sound check, Jerry Lee was upset that the upright piano was out of tune and ordered the sound man to "get that thing tuned up" before the show. About an hour before curtain time, Jerry Lee came on stage to test the piano, found the tuning not to his liking and pushed that piano right off the edge of the stage, smashing it to pieces! The crew scurried to find another piano before show time, and after the concert was over, the mood was crazy backstage because apparently, Jerry Lee had taken off in the promoter's jet with the promoter's girlfriend!

Note: When I was flying home a couple of days later, I noticed that Jerry Lee was on my flight to Nashville. I re-booked for a later flight. I didn't want to chance being on the same airplane, not with his karmic payback a possibility.

Someday I'm Gonna Rent This Town

···

CHAPTER 15

Working at the Airport, Yea

In spite of the action I was starting to get with my songs, the money truck wasn't exactly pulling up to my front door, so I took a job at the Nashville airport from midnight until 8 in the morning, sitting in one of those little aluminum booths in long term parking. I would take a reel-to-reel tape recorder and guitar to work and write songs all night. The booth had a pleasing natural echo to it and I started nine or ten songs a week out there. I began the songs *Forgive & Forget, We Can't Go On Living Like This* and *I Can't Help Myself* in that little aluminum booth, songs that later Eddie and I co-wrote and became some of the first hits for him as an artist.

Soon I was bringing in demos of our songs with Eddie singing the vocals and David Malloy got the idea that he would like to try his hand at producing, and capture in the studio some of the magic Eddie and I made at home. We began recording late at night, with David bringing in different players to supplement the guitar and vocals that Eddie would lay down. After completing six or seven cuts, he played the songs for Russ Regan of Elektra Records and Eddie Rabbitt, the artist, was signed. In 1975 the first release was Eddie's song *You Get To Me* which made the top thirty, followed by our co-written songs, *Forgive and Forget* and *I Should Have Married You.* Those records went to numbers 12 and 11 respectively. We were on our way, and we buckled down to write album number two, armed with a reason to write the very best material we could. We wrote over forty songs from which to choose.

When Eddie's first album was released we had a great laugh at the cover the label picked. It was a picture of him holding, what else but a rabbit. Unfortunately, the rabbit was too rambunctious at the photo shoot and had to be medicated so heavily that he looks dead as a doorknob lying in Eddie's lap. The album cover is now somewhat of a collector's item since the label re-released it in later years with a different cover altogether.

In making Eddie Rabbitt records, we found we sometimes couldn't make the songs feel quite as good in the studio as our home-made demos. Although the audio quality and musicianship was much better, the raw energy just wasn't there. We took great pains and time to refer back to the demos and get it to have that simple magic. In Nashville in those days, you were expected to get at least five or six songs recorded in a three hour session. We felt that was the wrong thing to do, which flew in the face of convention and the Nashville method of making albums in the mid 70's. Most albums had one, or at most, two hits with filler in between. Of course, you can't always write a hit, but we tried.

Eddie's career couldn't have begun any better, and he became the flagship of the Elektra country roster. It seemed as if the three of us could do no wrong. Eddie started calling us the "Trinity," which frankly, coming from my preacher kid background, made me a bit uneasy.

The Nashville branch of Elektra Records consisted of one man and a lovely assistant named Kitty. That man was Mike Suttle, a former independent record promoter. He was a *great* promo man and worked our records like there was no tomorrow. He wouldn't take no for an answer. Since there was no staff to speak of, no committees could be formed, therefore we had the luxury of picking what singles we wanted to pull from the albums. If David, Eddie, and I all thought we had a hit, Elektra released it, and I'll have to say, we had a great track record, with each new record scoring higher than the last on the charts.

CHAPTER 16

....

Lynn and Seth

From hanging out in clubs and playing pass-the-hat gigs, I met and became friends with a popular local rock group who called themselves "Peace & Quiet." Made up of unknowns, but future session players and record producers, the band consisted of talent such as Garth Fundis, the eventual and renowned producer of Don Williams, Keith Whitley, Trisha Yearwood and Sugarland fame, Spady Brannon, bassist and Biff Watson, acoustic guitarist, who have played on hits by Toby Keith, Shania Twain, Keith Urban, Martina McBride and Carrie Underwood, and Chris Leuzinger, guitarist on virtually all the Garth Brooks' records.

The boys in Peace & Quiet invited me to a house off West End Avenue that they shared and rehearsed in, and it was there that I met and fell in love with a lovely girl named Lynn Grady, at the time a bank teller at the local Third National Bank. After dating for quite a long time, I talked her into moving into my duplex with me. It was during our first months together that she became pregnant with my wonderful son, Seth, and what a beautiful little bundle of joy he was!

Jim Malloy suggested that we get a nicer place to live and he arranged for us to rent a big stone house right on Music Row's 16th Avenue where we set up our publishing company office and I began learning the ins and outs of the business of music publishing. When I wasn't writing songs I was doing the important paperwork that comes with professional songwriting and publishing. Lynn and I treasured our time together there watching our wonderful little boy grow up.

One night when Seth was about six months old I got him down on the floor, tickled him and recorded his great infectious laugh. Jim and I went into the studio and made a record of a song I had written about the wonders of having a child, *Let The Little Boy Dream*. We placed my recording of Seth's laugh on the introduction, instrumental break and ending of the song and Elektra released it as my new single as an artist to country radio. It climbed the charts into the top thirty and I was invited to play it on the Grand Ole Opry! What an honor that was! There I stood on the very stage, where Hank Williams, Dolly Parton, Merle Haggard, Willie Nelson and other legends had stood, singing my song with a recording of my little boy laughing for the audience and WSM Radio broadcasting it across the South and beyond. I think that Seth officially became the youngest performing artist on the Opry stage and probably on recorded vinyl as well!

CHAPTER 17

....

My Recording Career

By signing my recording contract with Elektra Records I became label mates with Eddie.

Shel Silverstein and I were hanging out and writing constantly during this time and Shel offered to help me put an album together which Jim and David Malloy produced at the popular studio, Quadraphonics.

Eclectic would be a fit description of my album. There was a country tune written with Eddie called *Delta Queen*, about a real riverboat on the Ohio River. Eddie sang harmony on that particular cut. There was a romping gospel medley that I wrote with Eddie, my father, Floyd, and my sister Sandy. Gospel group, The Oak Ridge Boys graciously sang on the song, *A Piece of the Rock*. My dad sang *Joshua Fit de Battle of Jericho* and my sister played organ on the cut. The Oaks, up to that time, were a full-fledged very famous gospel group, but signed with ABC Records the day after they sang on my album and became a pure country act with the album, "Y'all Come Back Saloon." Sherry Grooms and I sang a duet, written by Shel called, *The King of Country Music Meets The Queen of Rock & Roll*, with the Oaks singing backup on that as well. I let the truth be known when I sang the autobiographical song, *I'm From Outer Space*, another number I wrote with Shel. There were a couple of other quirky Shel tunes, *Vanilla* and *Come In Out'a The Sun*, co-written with Chris Gantry, but my favorite cut was a song that Shel and I wrote titled, *Too Many Nights Alone*.

Left to Right:
David Malloy, Shel Silverstein, Jim Malloy, Eddie Rabbitt, myself, Duane Allen, William Lee Golden, Richard Sturben, Joe Bonsall recording my Elektra album "Thorn" On The Rose".

Through no fault of their own, Elektra didn't have a clue how to market my album I called "A Thorn On The Rose," though I made an all-out effort to promote it by committing to an extensive radio station tour that ended up making me nuts. After three weeks on the road with various regional promotion men, I had an epiphany one night in a hotel room in New York. I realized that I hadn't written any songs in a month and it was making me miserable.

That night a rep from the label informed me that in four months, on October 8th, I was booked in Montgomery, Alabama, and it suddenly occurred to me, "I may not want to be in Montgomery, Alabama on October 8th!" I called Steve Wax, the president of Elektra Records and asked him if he would release me from the label. He said, "I've never had this call before!" but yes, they would release me if that's what I wanted. I hung up the phone and the weight of the world fell off of my shoulders. Looking back, I'm glad that I tried the artist thing. I got it out of my system and it gave me a clear vision of the life I wanted to live - the creative and free life of a songwriter - no boss, no timetables.

Unfortunately, things began to unravel for Lynn and I and she had a desire to move to Warm Springs, Georgia, where her mother lived. We both agreed that Seth would be better off growing up and going to school in that rural environment. At that point in my song-writing career, I knew I had to stay living and working in Nashville. We had an amicable separation and I made a point of getting down to Georgia every weekend I could, and Seth spent every summer with me until he graduated from high school. I guess it all worked out for the best, because Seth turned out so great, but to this day I regret the times I wasn't there for him. I sure loved and missed that kid when he was gone, and shed many a tear driving back to Nash-ville each time I had to take him back to his Mom's house in Georgia.

On the strength of the success of album number one, there was more time and money to spend on Eddie Rabbitt's next album. It was called *Rocky Mountain Music*. More budget meant more free-dom to experiment and refine our recordings. One of the hardest core country songs Eddie and I ever wrote became the first release and our first full-fledged number one hit, *Drinkin' My Baby (Off Of My Mind)*.

Number one! Lord, were we excited! Then came the para-noia of following up. Elektra released the title song, *Rocky Mountain Music* next and the flip side was a song I co-wrote with Eddie called *Do You Right Tonight*. Radio began playing both sides and we ended up having a double-sided number one Billboard hit . . . two country hits for the price of one, a very rare occurrence, also entering the Billboard Pop chart for the first time at number one . . . Sweet indeed.

At this point Eddie figured it was time to form a serious road band and get out there to promote his records. He auditioned and rehearsed until he was satisfied with the musicians and named his backup group Hare Trigger. It consisted of, at various times, Jimmy Hyde on drums and vocals, Don Barrett on bass and vocals, Gene Sisk on keyboards and vocals, Michael Spriggs and Lee Garner on guitars, Andy Byrd on keyboards, Ned Davis on steel guitar and vo-cals, and John Paul Daniel on guitars and vocals. Also brought on board was Bill Rehrig as Road Manager, a mellow soul and excellent fiddle player, who added a down home touch to Eddie's roadshow.

Working the road is an expensive proposition. Renting buses, hiring a road manager, paying a band year round (to avoid an off season mutiny), hotel rooms, food and a hundred other expenses can sure add up. It's a financial treadmill that's hard to jump off of. Eddie used to claim that he lost around ten thousand dollars every time he went on stage until he had two or three number one records under his belt.

Elektra came next with a song Eddie wrote on his own, titled *Two Dollars In The Jukebox*, a hard country rocker that peaked at number three on the Billboard chart. In the spring of 1977 they came with another song Eddie and I wrote called, *I Can't Help Myself,* an idea I first conceived in that little aluminum parking attendant booth back at the airport. It peaked at number two on the charts, fighting Waylon Jennings, with guest vocal by Willie Nelson, and the great song, *Luckenbach, Texas (Back to the Basics of Love)* for the number one spot that week. Pretty great company, I'd say. Our release was strong on the country and pop charts and burned up the radio for sixteen weeks, which is always a good thing. Songwriters love it when their songs have a long run on the radio. One of the major ways we are paid for our services is for the airplay that a song racks up. At that time, I believe we earned a little over five cents per play and the longer you were on the charts, the more money you made.

CHAPTER 18

······································

Shel Silverstein

1977 was a very good year. Not only was I having consistent hits as a songwriter, but it was the year I met my friend, Shel Silverstein.

Driving down 16th Avenue on Music Row one morning, I saw a strange, out-of-place looking dude on the sidewalk. I recognized him from his photos in Playboy, and had always admired his drawings and his songs. Shel had already written the classics, *A Boy Named Sue* by Johnny Cash, *Cover of The Rolling Stone* and *Sylvia's Mother* by Dr. Hook. I pulled up beside him and said, "Hey Shel, would you like a ride?" Little did I know that was the start of a friendship that lasted until the day he passed away, with a wonderful, unique person and a giant of creativity. We hit it off immediately, writing five songs that very first day, of which three ended up being recorded by major recording artists! Our first hit came that summer with a top fifteen charter on the lovely Stella Parton called, *The Danger of A Stranger*.

To give an example of just how prolific Shel was, one night after a day of songwriting, I let Shel out of my truck in front of his hotel, with plans of picking him back up early the next morning for more writing. When I knocked on his door the next day, he opened it to a room strewn with scores of drawings and writings from his night of creativity. I asked, "What's all that?" to which he replied, "Oh, it's a new book I wrote last night." He gathered up a pile of papers saying, "Take these home and let me know if it's any good or not." That pile of papers ended up being his classic children's book, "A Light In The Attic," a brilliant piece of work.

That's how Shel was, always writing, always thinking and creating. We hung out not only in Nashville, but at his house in Key West, apartment in Greenwich Village and his houseboat in Sausalito. We wrote slews of songs together and it was always so much fun.

Rewind:

Hillary Kanter, a frequent song writing partner of mine, and I were once in the Caribbean, and while walking down a path nearly got conked on the head by a coconut. That inspired a song idea called *Killed By A Coconut* . . . the premise being that this fictitious fellow spent all his life eating healthy food, exercising religiously, getting to bed early, etc., only to be killed by a falling coconut. We were at Shel's house in Key West months later and mentioned the idea to him. He got very excited and said he wanted to write, "some verses" to that idea. When we came back the next day he had about fifteen different verses written about the many ways a person can be killed by the lowly coconut and each one was fantastic. That song can be heard recorded by the legendary folk artist, Bob Gibson on his CD, "Makin' A Mess" on the Elektra label. Bob was a major figure of the folk music revival in the late 1950's and early 1960's. His songs have been recorded by Peter Paul & Mary, Simon & Garfunkel, The Byrds, The Smothers Brothers and The Kingston Trio.

Having Shel as a friend was so rewarding. One day he said he wanted me to meet his friend Bobby Bare, so we drove over to a new office Bobby was moving into on Music Row. The office was bare except for one chair. When we arrived, some workers were just finishing tacking down some new beige shag carpeting. After being introduced, Bobby picked up his guitar and started playing us this new song he was excited about. In those days Bobby always had a wad of tobacco between his lip and gum and as he sang his song, it became obvious that he had to spit. Instead of stopping the song, Bobby just spat that goop out on the new carpet between verses, never missing a beat. I thought that was about the coolest move I had ever seen. It was more important to him not to mess up the flow of the song than to mess up the new carpeting! I loved that guy from that day forward, and he recorded some of my songs through the years, including a great version of *Too Many Nights Alone*.

Truth is, Shel introduced me to many super people. It was through Shel that I met Brenda Lee, the boys in Dr. Hook, John Hartford and the soulful Lacy J. Dalton, who has become my dear friend.

I was with Shel in Key West just a week before his passing, and he was still generous. He felt that I should be writing stories for kids and we had plans of getting together soon so that he could show me the ropes. Sorry to say, I never got to have that experience and I sure was looking forward to learning from the master . . . the man who wrote such books as "The Giving Tree," "Where The Sidewalk Ends" and other iconic literary wonders.

1977 ended with another top ten in Eddie Rabbitt's career, *We Can't Go On Living Like This*. A song co-written with Eddie about "just going through the motions" in a played-out love affair.

Shel and I writing songs.

1978 started with a bang and never let up. In the early spring they released, *Hearts On Fire*, we co-wrote with Dan Tyler, one of our publishing company's writers. It flew up the charts and stayed at number one for a couple of weeks, followed in the summer by another number one Country and number 55 Pop hit, *You Don't Love Me Anymore*, a fantastic song we published by our good friend Alan Ray and his co-writer, Jeff Raymond. In the autumn, our song, *I Just Want To Love You*, co-written with David Malloy and put together from bits of different song ideas we had, also hit number one. Then, just after Christmas, Eddie had a monster with the theme song for a Clint Eastwood movie, *Every Which Way But Loose*, an outside project, written for the movie by Steve Dorff, Milton Brown, and Snuff Garrett. It stayed at number one for three weeks and also went top thirty on the pop chart. I went with Eddie to the premier showing of that movie. We sat there, very excited to hear Ed kick off the Clint Eastwood film with his recording but when it came on the house speakers something was terribly wrong, and the sound came out loud and distorted, and Eddie just looked at me and shook his head sadly.

Rewind:

When Clint Eastwood asked Eddie Rabbitt to sing *Every Which Way But Loose* for the movie of the same name, we flew out to Los Angeles together for a gig Eddie had booked at the Palomino. Clint Eastwood showed up in the audience, along with his girl friend, Sondra Locke. After the gig, Eddie and I were writing on a song in his hotel room when there was a knock on the door, and there stood Clint and Sondra, big as life. We had a great visit together and Clint Eastwood was exactly like you would hope he would be . . . down to earth with a great sense of humor. To my surprise, Sondra Locke kept complimenting me on my songwriting and knew the words to some of my more obscure cuts. She was a real fan. Sometimes you never know what surprises could be standing right outside your door.

Eddie came off the road that holiday season and we set out to write another album's-worth of songs. We were hell bent on keeping this number streak going and we dove in head first into the writing process. We rented a couple of rooms at the Spence Manor hotel on Music Row and rocked out for weeks, cranking out what we hoped were new hits. When we had a handful written, we would go into our little publishing studio, The Garage, and make our mini-record demos of the songs, laying out the blueprint for upcoming master sessions with cream of the crop musicians. Then, back into our hide-away, writing incessantly until we knew we had the goods.

Someday I'm Gonna Rent This Town

CHAPTER 19

....

Wood Newton

1978 was the year I began officially producing records. My first act was a wonderful singer and songwriter named Wood Newton. He was introduced to me by the aforementioned and fine songwriter, Dan Tyler. The very first time I met Wood I liked the guy. He was an Arkansas native and had a kind and straight forward way about him, and a voice that was unique, warm and real. We had a great time making his first album with some of the stellar musicians in Nashville. We had piano man Hargus "Pig" Robbins, lead guitarist, Danny Stockard, the late harmonica giant, Terry McMillan, Buddy Spicher, Scotty Saunders, Buster Phillips, Jack Williams, and vocal

Jim Malloy, Me & Wood Newton

backup by our friends Sherry Grooms and Paul Overstreet. Wood's singles got up there in the 40's and 50's with the songs *Last Exit For Love* and *Lock, Stock & Barrel*, but one of my favorite's was *Dreams of Desiree* which I wrote with Dan Tyler and Wood sang with that cool, earthy voice of his. Another true friend made.

CHAPTER 20

....

Enter Dr. Hook

I was ecstatic with my song writing career, but things were about to go from cruising in a jet at 30,000 feet to a rocket ride into the stratosphere! My successes up to this point were mostly Country with occasional cross overs into the Pop and Adult Contemporary charts, but I was also writing pop, rock and R&B music that I had a hard time getting recorded in Nashville.

One of those non-country songs I wrote was *When You're In Love With A Beautiful Woman*.

One night I was standing at the bar in The Commodore Lounge at the Holiday Inn near Vanderbilt University waiting for my new girlfriend, Sherry Grooms, to take her break from singing on stage with a cover band. She was making her way over to me, but guys in the audience kept stopping her and hitting on her until she had to go back up to sing. Well, that pissed me off so I left, and as I drove the fifteen minutes or so back to my apartment I wrote that song. When I got home I picked up my guitar and somehow just knew what chords should be played and sat back and went from irked to elated, thinking, "I know I just wrote a hit song!"

I had a favorite uncle named Jack, my mother's brother, who happened to be one of Engelbert Humperdinck's greatest friends. Over the years he had mentioned to me that I should send him some songs to pitch to Engelbert, but I never did because it just felt awkward. But when I wrote *When You're In Love With A Beautiful Woman* I thought, "This song could really fit Engelbert and be a major hit for him." I was sure it was a good follow-up song for recent hits he was famous for like *After The Lovin'*. I called Jack and he said, "well, fly on out here and you can play it in person for Engelbert."

I booked a studio and the great session guitarist, Jimmy Capps, and upright bassist, Billy Linneman, to record a simple demo of my song and then booked a flight to LA.

Uncle Jack met me at the airport and drove me to the Beverly Hills Hotel where we met up with Engelbert and had a few drinks. On the way to his house we stopped at a pub or two and drank a little more and played a few games of darts. I sucked at the game, but Engelbert was a master dart-man and whipped Jack and I every time. Finally we pulled into his humble abode, the former mansion of Jayne Mansfield on Sunset Boulevard, next door to Cher's spread. His house was incredible, with thirteen bathrooms, a living room the size Texas, containing the actual grand piano once owned by George Gershwin, on which he had written, *Rhapsody In Blue*. There was a huge fountain in the middle of the room and the water flowed from it and went under the floor and outside, where it ran down a river into the heart-shaped swimming pool that Jayne Mansfield had designed for herself. I could just imagine a bikini-clad Jayne lounging there in all her splendor. I was more than a little blown away by his house since I lived in a single-wide trailer in Mount Juliet, Tennessee at the time . . . just a bit out of my element! Pretty damn impressive!

After a tour of the house, Engelbert said, "I hear you've written a song that you want me to think about recording. Let's go down to the rec room and listen. I just put in a 15,000 dollar sound system, so your tape should sound great." I handed my reel-to-reel tape to him and he threaded it onto his tape recorder and pressed "play." We heard only the first five notes of the introduction and suddenly his player ate my tape! He said, "Your tape's ruined my machine!" I said, "Your machine is destroying my tape!"

So that was that. I hadn't brought my guitar with me on the trip, so I told Engelbert that I would try to send him a copy of the song when I got home. I left Los Angeles dejected and depressed, thinking I had blown a big chance.

The day after I got home I ran into my buddy, Shel, and he told me that Dr. Hook was in the process of recording a new album and that he had played them all his new material and that they didn't think it was quite right for their project. He said, "Eve, I think you might be writing exactly what they are after. How 'bout I bring their producer, Ron Haffkine, by the studio to hear some of your songs?" Shel, of course, was known for many of Dr. Hook's signature songs. He wrote, *Sylvia's Mother, Got Stoned and I Missed It, Freakin' At The Freaker's Ball, Cover of the Rolling Stone* and scores of other songs that made Dr. Hook a household name. Of course I said yes, and that I, coincidently, was recording the next day. I was putting some background vocals on *When You're In Love With A Beautiful Woman* with Sherry when they arrived at the studio. After a few minutes of listening, Ron Haffkine freaked over the song and asked me to "put it on hold" because he thought it was a "big smash" for Dr. Hook.

I was invited down the next week to Muscle Shoals, Alabama for Dr. Hook's recording session at the old Jackson Highway Recording Studio and it will always live as a magic few days in my life. First of all, Dr. Hook was recording with the creme de la creme of all musicians, the Muscle Shoals Rhythm Section, made up of Jimmy Johnson on electric guitar, Barry Beckett on keys, Roger Hawkins on drums and David Hood on bass. These guys had played on hundreds of hits by the very best: Aretha Franklin, Bob Seger, Paul Simon, The Rolling Stones, etc. Add to that other greats who added licks on my song were musicians, Pete Carr, Larry Byrom, Randy McCormick, Tom Roady, Mickey Buckins and Kenneth Bell. The background vocals were sung by The Cherry Sisters, Lisa Silver, Sheri Kramer and Diane Tidwell, and the strings were arranged and conducted by Mike Lewis, famed for his work with the Bee Gees. Man, I was walking in tall cotton!

I had written this song in a slow groove, with a Smokey Robinson sort of feel. When Dr. Hook began recording I was a bit put off by the way the tempo was sped up, but by about the third listen or so I was on board and loving every minute of it. I left Muscle Shoals, Alabama with no doubt that I had a real big hit on my hands.

That summer, *When You're In Love With A Beautiful Woman* became gold or platinum in thirteen countries, setting records in Great Britain for staying three weeks at number one. It seemed to be on the lips of everyone and on every Rock and Pop station on the radio dial.

Rewind:

A rare moment I will never forget: Sherry, the girl that the song was written about, and I flew to Bermuda for some fun in the sun. We grabbed a cab for the ride to our hotel, and as we motored across the island, our driver, right out of the blue, started singing *When You're In Love With A Beautiful Woman*, totally unaware that the author, and the girl the song was written about, was sitting in the backseat of his cab. I just sat there with a big grin on my face thinking, "It truly doesn't get any better than this."

During the time *When You're In Love With a Beautiful Woman* began it's way to the top of the charts, Norbert Putnam, the man who once told me to "go back to Ohio" invited me to fly down to the island of Montserrat to hang out and watch Jimmy Buffett record his new album that was released as *Volcano*.

They were recording in George Martin's mountaintop, Air Studio. Gene Eichelberger, the engineer that recorded my Elektra album, *Thorn On The Rose* was there, along with Geoff Emerick, the chief engineer for the majority of the Beatles' hits. Everyone was in a party mood, running around with their hand on top of their heads, imitating sharks. I thought they were all nuts until I caught on to the song they were recording, a song called *Fins*. "*You got Fins to the left of you, Fins to the right, And you're the only bait in town!*" What a fun bunch. That first evening, Jimmy had "the world's greatest steel drummer" play beautiful songs like Mona Lisa while we ate gourmet food laid out on big, beautiful tables outside on the patio, as the sun set over the Caribbean sea. Old Jimmy Buffett knows how to live!

While on the island I met the whole Taylor clan: James, Alex, and Livingston. They were there, adding vocals to the Buffett album. Alex was exceptionally fun to be around, but James seemed a bit off-ish. It was exciting hanging out at George Martin's studio in paradise, thanks to my buddy, Norbert.

One month later Eddie released our song *Suspicions* . . . All the stars were aligned!

Someday I'm Gonna Rent This Town

CHAPTER 21

....

Suspicions

How the song, *Suspicions* came to be written was a great surprise. David, Eddie, and I had been content with recording in Nashville studios, but it dawned on us that maybe it was time to plow more fertile ground, studio wise. During the many months that Eddie was out working the road, David and I were involved in other individual projects and some of those things meant traveling and working at other studios in other cities. The next Eddie Rabbitt album, "Loveline," was recorded in Muscle Shoals, Los Angeles, and Nashville, using players and studios from all of those places.

On a lunch break, while recording tracks at Wally Heider's Studio in Los Angeles, we wrote one of Eddie Rabbitt's biggest hits.

The Muscle Shoals Rhythm Section had flown out for a week of tracking and we were wrapping up the last days of recording. All the players had left the building for lunch except Eddie, David, myself, and keyboardist Randy McCormick. Randy sat down in the middle of the studio and began doodling on a groove at the Rhodes piano. We pulled up some stools and began throwing out melody and lyric ideas and within a half-hour or so we had the essence of a song we were calling *Suspicions*. David called into the control room for the engineer, Peter Granet, to turn on some type of tape to capture a rough take of our new song. Just at that moment, drummer Roger Hawkins came back from lunch and sat down at the drums and started improvising along as we recorded our work demo. When we finished, we were whoopin' and hollerin', "man, that was great sounding, did you get that down Peter?" He came back over the intercom with, "Not only did I get it, but I recorded it on the 24 track master tape and I got the drums down too!" Well, that little work tape ended up being so magic that we spent all of that evening and well into the night tweaking the lyrics and getting a final vocal from Eddie before he had to catch a flight for some gig. Later, David Hungate, from the group Toto, came in and laid down the perfect bass part, the legendary Ernie Watts added the flute solo, Tim May the electric guitar, and Steve Forman, the perfect percussion. The icing on the cake was Randy McCormick's innovative string arrangement. Thanks to good luck and a sharp recording engineer, we caught the genie in the bottle.

Suspicions became a hit, not only on the Country charts, but also Pop and Adult Contemporary as well. We won the coveted Robert J. Burton Award from BMI that year as the "Most Played Country Song" and *Suspicions* set the stage for a string of crossover hits to come.

Photo for Robert J. Burton Award - BMI Most Played Song of the Year Suspicions. Left to Right: Randy McCormick, David Malloy, Eddie Rabbitt and yours truly.

CHAPTER 22

....

Eddie Rabbitt's Monkey

While Ed was out working the road, I spent my time writing and pitching songs to other artists, producers and A&R people at the record companies. When he was in town, usually from November to sometime in the spring, we spent every waking moment writing, demoing and stockpiling songs for his next album. I suppose if you were a fly on the wall, our writing process would have seemed rather bizarre. I don't believe we ever wrote a song without the television on in the background. We used to call it our "little friend," a source for ideas and serving as a time filler when we were stumped. We watched many a soap opera in those days with Eddie's capuchin monkey, JoJo, hopping around the furniture like the little wild beast that he was. JoJo was a freaky little critter, and I was about the only other human being that Ed could let him out of his cage around, without JoJo going bananas and biting somebody. I had my share of days when he would sneak up behind me and pull my hair out by the paw-full. He was always a pain in the ass, but could be entertaining at times.

JoJo had his own little television right outside of his cage, and when it was feeding time, he would stuff his food into the top of the torn off head of a rubber Shoney's Big Boy doll and hunker down to watch his favorite TV programs. He definitely had his favorites. For example, he knew when it was Saturday evening and time for Hee Haw . . . he *loved* that show. I guess that's some indication of the caliber of humor they were going for. He also was smitten with Johnny Carson and would go absolutely nuts when Johnny came walking out from behind that curtain to do his monologue. Of course, JoJo had a few disgusting habits. Whenever any beautiful blonde girl came on the tube, he'd get a wild and crazy look in his eye, round up his blanket, get comfy and proceed to stare at the TV and . . . masturbate.

One weekend, Eddie's Irish mother came to visit from New Jersey. We were all sitting around having some libations while JoJo slept peacefully in his cage in the corner of the living room. Just then the banjo theme song for Hee Haw came on and JoJo shot straight up from his sleep and started rattling the bars on his cage and screeching his ear-piercing monkey sounds. Eddie's mom thought it was so "cute." Unfortunately, about five minutes into the show, on comes a blonde Hee Haw Honey and JoJo goes into his not-so-private routine. I was in the middle of taking a drink and did a spit take clear across the living room. Mom, of course, was in wide-eyed shock, and in her thickest Irish brogue said, "Oh Eddie, that's so *NASTY!*" running, mortified, from the room.

That wasn't the only Mom and JoJo incident. That following week, Eddie and I were under the earphones in the recording room. Mom decided to help out around the house and began dumping all the ashtrays into a garbage can. As her *lack* of Irish luck would have it, there was a still-burning cigarette in the bunch and it started the can on fire, which in turn caught the curtains on fire, which in turn caused smoke to come rolling out of the windows, fortunately seen by Eddie's next door neighbor, George, who came racing up the stairs and into the room shouting, "FIRE!" The whole apartment was full of smoke by that time, and while I dialed the fire department, Eddie Ran over and unlocked JoJo's cage. JoJo immediately ran screaming through the place until he saw George, whom he didn't like, and bit him on the hand. This triggered panic in George, for he had studied voodoo, and supposedly a monkey bite was very bad juju indeed. So here we had an apartment on fire, a berserk monkey, a hysterical mother, a freaked out, monkey-bit neighbor, and one furious Eddie Rabbitt. Me? I was mostly concerned about saving our demo tapes.

CHAPTER 23

On a Roll

After the fantastic success of *Suspicions*, Eddie, David, and I put our heads together to pick the next single release from the "Loveline" album. Our choices were either *Gone Too Far, Loveline,* or *I Don't Wanna Make Love (With Anyone Else But You)*, but the label kept insisting that we release *Pour Me Another Tequila*. We liked that song, but frankly, we never really considered it as our strongest single. The people at the label, and there were many, chimed in about the huge successes we were having. They warned us that we might lose our country following if we didn't follow *Suspicions* with, as they put it, something "less progressive." We reminded them that *Suspicions* had just been awarded "Country Song of the Year," but to no avail. So they had their way and *Pour Me Another Tequila* was released. It only went to number five. This was after we released four number one songs in a row. After that, the record company people bowed out and let us continue picking the singles.

The groove cut, *Gone Too Far* kicked off the spring of 1980 for Eddie Rabbitt, the artist, and for Eddie, David, and I as songwriters. That song was an exercise in simplicity, written in the car on our way down to Muscle Shoals for some sessions. I remember we had that car rocking and that two hour trip seemed like 30 minutes, we were having so much fun. Fortune again smiled on us with yet another number one chart topper.

Rewind: I Should Be Dead 4 Times Already

The first time was when I was 12 or 13. Quite often I rode my bike the five miles to Indian Lake to my friend Bobby Given's house. We decided to ride over to the bridge that overlooked the spillway and search for big fish underneath. Bobby was peering over one rail of the bridge and I over the other on the opposite side of the road when he yelled for me to "come quick." I turned on my heels and ran out into the road, right into the path of a speeding automobile. I remember Bobby's wide eyes, the sound of squealing tires, and the big chrome front end of a Buick. That driver squealed to a stop not a moment too soon. I bounced harmlessly off of his front grille . . . a couple seconds later and I would have been dead meat.

My second brush with the grim reaper involved a logging truck. My dad bought the old house across the street from ours and hired me and my buddy, Stevie Jenkins, to clean it out and take the junk to the dump. Stevie brought over his dad's Ford tractor with a two-wheeled trailer hitched to the back. We loaded it up with an old iron stove, refrigerator, and some useless furniture, and with him driving, and me sitting on the tongue, with my back against the trailer, we headed out of town down a country road. I had a transistor radio to my ear, as we approached a sharp curve. Halfway through the curve I looked up and an enormous yellow truck fender was speeding right towards me. I guess I moved out of the way just in time, because the next thing I knew I was lying in a field, on the other side of a fence, with stove and fridge and pieces of trailer scattered all around me. That logging truck demolished that trailer, leaving only the axle and two wheels recognizable. I still had the radio in my hand and the only damage to me was a gash on my forehead and the ass end of my jeans torn out. I later found out a one-eyed guy had been driving the truck.

The third time wasn't charming at all. A girlfriend tried to stab me with a steak knife. I guess it should have come as no surprise, she was always a little on the crazy side . . . but that's what I liked about her. We used to get hot and heavy in the dining room on the piano bench while her parents watched I Love Lucy in the next room. We had a rather tumultuous love affair, always accusing each other of infidelity (which was true), and other lurid teenage behavior, but she was the first truly uninhibited female I had ever met, and I was willing to put up with about anything for that wild stuff. One New Year's Eve she threw a party at her apartment and everybody got real drunk. As the last people stumbled out of the door, this cute girl turned and gave me a big kiss. My girlfriend didn't take it too well. She was upset and sat on the back of the couch, chug-a-luggin' a fifth of Jim Beam. I was in the kitchen, trying to make her a much-needed cup of coffee. I turned around just in time to catch the descending arm of a crazed maniac with a steak knife in hand. I stopped that knife about a half inch from my left eye. I ended up with a death grip on her wrist, flailing around the room like Duke Wayne fending off some liquored-up Apache. Of course, we made up and sealed the misunderstanding with some great sex. After all, she wasn't really trying to kill me, just blind me. Things were a bit paranoid on my end from that day forward in that ill fated relationship.

It was while living in Carmel, California that I about "Bit the Big One" for the fourth time. I was on my way up the coast to San Francisco in my Volkswagen bus, looking forward to a Jefferson Airplane concert at the Fillmore. I had a homemade pipe and five chunks of primo Lebanese blonde hash in my shirt pocket. About twenty miles into the trip, I stopped to pick up a hippie with a sign that read "Fillmore." He was a pleasant enough fellow and it wasn't long before we were smoking hashish and he was adding his ground up peyote buttons to the pipe. We were in quite a heightened state of consciousness when all hell broke loose. A sixteen year old kid in a pickup truck came speeding down a side road to my left, ran the stop sign and I hit his truck broadside at about fifty miles an hour. It all happened so fast, I didn't even have time to get my foot off the gas. It was daylight when I hit him, but it was nighttime when I came to, lying in a pool of blood and glass, with my feet still hung up in the pedals of the bus. There was a priest making Catholic signs and gibbering something above me, with flashing red lights everywhere. I knew I was alive, but I had no clue *what* had happened, *where I* was, or *who* I was . . . I had total amnesia. They loaded me into an ambulance and on the way over the hills to a San Francisco hospital I began having memory flashes like Albert DeSalvo had in the movie, The Boston Strangler. First I remembered that I was in the Coast Guard. A few minutes later I remembered the hitch hiker. Then I remembered my name, and finally, I remembered I had *four grams of highly illegal hashish in my shirt pocket!* I was told there would be a police man meeting me at the emergency room to take an accident report, so I did the only thing one can do in such a situation . . . I quietly unwrapped the hashish from under the blanket, and while the ambulance attendant was distracted, I slipped all four chunks into my mouth, chewed and swallowed. By the time we reached the hospital, I was really flying high. A doctor sewed up the big windshield-wiper-looking gash in my head, and I swear I could hear that needle squeaking through my scalp with every stitch. A wave of nausea swept over me and I threw up a porridge of hashish stew worth about two hundred bucks. Somehow I got through the police interview by answering "Yes sir, No sir" over and over, while his face did rubbery psychedelic tricks in front of me. I healed up all right, but that episode of amnesia still haunts me. For an hour or so I absolutely had no future, present or past.

According to the police man, witnesses said that right after the accident, the hitch hiker ran over, looked down at me and said, "Shit, he's dead!", and ran off down the road, never to be heard from again. What a caring Love Child he was. The teenager who ran the stop sign recovered from a broken leg and major contusions, his learner's permit was revoked, and his insurance company paid me a few thousand dollars for a new old bus. What I really wanted was reimbursed for all that righteous Lebanese blonde hashish that went to waste!

CHAPTER 24

The Eddie Rabbitt Sound

As anyone would know just from listening to Eddie Rabbitt's records, harmonies were an important part of his sound. We were of one mind when it came to this subject. Eddie and I sometimes used to have to duke it out with David about how much, how often, and how loud the harmonies needed to be on a record. David was of the "less is more" school and Eddie and I were on the "more is more" side of the harmony controversy. We believed that harmony had a way of connecting on a gut level with people, touching not only their heads and their hearts, but also their very guts, and deeper regions as well.

I recon that back in cave man times, one night, Oggg was hunkered down over the campfire, humming a little tune, when Augg joined in and suddenly hit a note that made them both stand erect and smile. The first discovery of two part harmony . . . wouldn't surprise me if they didn't go searching the countryside for someone to sing the high lonesome part. Harmony is a beautiful thing.

Another crucial part of the Eddie Rabbitt sound was the rhythm acoustic guitar. When we wrote songs we would have a ball playing them over and over just to hear that tight sound of our two guitars jiving up perfectly. Though Eddie endorsed Ovation guitars and played one on stage, he seldom used one while writing. He did his song writing on this nondescript old gut string with butterfly decals all over it. It was pretty sick, but it worked for him. When we made records, he always played the acoustic tracks on my guitar, a steel string Takamine. Eddie could beat the hell out of a guitar. Check out the playing on *Drivin' My Life Away*. My guitar was the only one that sounded robust enough and could take the punishment. I had to have that thing operated on after every album but it hung in there through most of his whole career.

CHAPTER 25

....

Platinum

In the summer of 1980 we got a call from Steve Wax, the former head of Elektra Records, now in charge of finding movie music for Warner Brothers Pictures. He asked us to write a song for the soundtrack of an upcoming movie titled, "The Roadie." It starred the rock star, Meatloaf and Art Carney, you know, Norton, of TV's The Honeymooners fame. We had an eight track Tascam recorder in the attic of our publishing company and Eddie, David, and I spent days up there carving out a tune that we thought would work for the film. As we wrote it, we began to realize that one hell of a song was being created. We talked Elektra into letting us use the song on not only the movie soundtrack, but also on the upcoming Eddie Rabbitt album, titled "Horizon." Thank goodness, because *Drivin' My Life Away* caught on like Coca Cola and zoomed up the charts, setting an all-time record for entering the country charts at the highest level, never surpassed until many years later by Garth Brooks. The promotion team even told us that they had to slow it down from going to the top too fast, so we could get more weeks of airplay. *Drivin' My Life Away* gave us a number one Country hit, a top five single hit on Billboard's Hot 100 pop chart and our first million-selling single and platinum album. The movie itself was forgettable, but the soundtrack album was happening, with great cuts by Teddy Pendergrass, Pat Benatar, Blondie, Cheap Trick, Jerry Lee Lewis, Styx and my particular favorite, *That Loving You Feelin*, a duet by Emmylou Harris and Roy Orbison.

Most of the Horizon album was recorded at Caribou Ranch,

near Nederland, Colorado. What a place that was to record. Situated in the Rocky Mountains and owned by James Guercio, the producer of the group Blood, Sweat and Tears, Chicago and later the creator of CMT/Country Music Television. Caribou had state of the art recording facilities, a dining hall, four or five historic cabins scattered around the three thousand acre property and afforded it's clients a beautiful remote spot to hole up and create music, free from the distractions of the real world. We would stay there for weeks at a time. My favorite cabin became Ouray, a small log house with an oversized bed that was custom made for bassist Stanley Clark. Evidently he was super tall. We wrote the hit *Step By Step* one morning in that cabin while I was cooking us some bacon and eggs.

As, was often the case, when we recorded the tracks for records that needed to be driven by Eddie's acoustic playing, I would sing the rough tracking vocal, since there would be guitar leakage in Eddie's vocal microphone if he tried to do both the guitar and sing at the same time. The recording of *Drivin' My Life Away* sticks in my memory as one of the most electrifying three minutes in my life. We ran it down a time or two, then Eddie kicked the song off perfectly with his rocking acoustic guitar. Larry Byrom, on electric guitar, had been sitting down during the run-throughs, but when it came time for his signature lead guitar work, I remember him rising from his chair and creating those signature chorus licks that still give me goose bumps whenever I hear that song on the radio. The air in that studio went liquid with magic.

We recorded some of Eddie's most successful albums at Caribou Ranch. The list of clients that stayed and recorded at that paradise ranged from Elton John's *Rock of the Westies*, Amy Grant 's *Unguarded*, Steve Martin's comedy albums, five Chicago albums, to Waylon Jennings and almost everyone else in between. Sequestered away from the world, sleeping in one hundred year old cabins, being well fed with hearty mountain grub, made for a great time. We made some of our best records, with some of the world's greatest musicians, up there high in those Rocky Mountains.

Eddie Rabbitt was many things, but an outdoorsman was not one of them. He and I were walking back to our cabins one snowy night, when off in the distance we heard a wolf howl. Remember, we were on a three thousand acre ranch in the middle of the Rocky Mountains. Eddie turned to me and said, in all seriousness, "I didn't know there was a zoo around here." Sometimes he cracked me up.

Someday I'm Gonna Rent This Town

CHAPTER 26

....

Rainy Nights

Three months later we scored with what has proved to be the biggest hit of Eddie Rabbitt's recording career. A feel good tune called, *I Love A Rainy Night*.

Eddie had this little 10 second snippet of an idea on an old cassette that he ran by David and I at writing sessions a couple of times in years past. We had always been oblivious to it's potential, but one night it started to click with us. I recall that David started snapping his fingers and clapping his hands while we were writing it. One of us said, "Yea, that's cool, keep that up . . . we should record it like that!" It's a wonder he didn't develop a serious case of carpal tunnel syndrome for he must have snapped and clapped for hours during the writing process. We went into the studio with a rough demo, but that song got a major reshaping once we started to make the record. We eliminated a bridge, extended the length of the hook and buffed up the lyrics until they shined. Most of one day was wasted with each of us trying to record four minutes of hand claps and finger snaps, but none of us could keep it sounding consistent. Finally, a percussionist, Farrell Morris, was brought in and he nailed it in a few passes. Super guitarist, Larry Byrom again played a simple but screaming electric guitar solo that never grows old to me. It's no wonder Larry came up with such fantastic guitar work, he was a member of the rock group Steppenwolf. For many years Larry has been one of the hottest and most inventive session men working in Muscle Shoals, Alabama, and Music City.

As *I Love A Rainy Night* was zooming up the Country, Adult Contemporary, and Hot 100 Pop Charts, one of the largest advertising companies in New York City called on behalf of their client, The Miller Brewing Company. They wanted us to write a series of Miller Beer commercials and they needed them fast. Eddie was busy working the road, doing television and radio promoting the record, so David and I flew to New York and spent three or four days composing the jingles for Eddie to sing. They became very successful radio ads for Miller Beer and ended up winning David and I the coveted "Big Apple Advertising Award" for our efforts. On the very week *I Love A Rainy Night* topped the Hot 100 Pop charts, Miller Beer released their nationwide television campaign featuring Eddie on stage singing our song. That helped propel it to stay at number one for an amazing three consecutive weeks on the Hot 100 Billboard pop chart!

Rewind:

When the career of Eddie Rabbitt was at it's peak, he found out that his name was involved in divorce proceedings in a far off state. Seems this female fan he had never met was so enamored with him that she was willing to risk losing it all because of her obsession. We had an office red alert warning out for this girl, who would appear every now and then on the steps of our publishing company, acting just plain nutty, wanting to see Eddie Rabbitt. The place would go into lockdown, because we did not want to take any chances. In court, her husband said that his wife spent all their money buying tickets and traveling to Eddie's concerts, no matter how far away. She had posters of Eddie above their bed and played his albums until her husband couldn't stand them anymore. She got her wish and lost him and both her kids in the divorce. Pure craziness, and what a pity. As Eddie used to say, "Sometimes, fan is short for fanatic."

CHAPTER 27

Europe

As *I Love A Rainy Night* was progressing up all the charts, Jim Malloy and I flew to London to meet with our sub-publishers, Terry & Mandy Oates, in England. Most of the day with Terry was spent at the local pub drinking pints of Guinness, while Mandy stayed back at their brownstone, the former office of Noel Coward, taking care of business . . . very nice people.

One evening they treated us to dinner and then we headed to the Royal Albert Hall, where Scottish comedian, Billy Connoly was headlining. It took about half an hour of listening to his thick Scottish brogue before I could really understand what he was saying, but I remember one particular joke of his. He said that sometimes he lays down with one arm under his back until it goes to sleep . . . then when he's abusing himself, it feels like someone else is doing it . . . Kind of gross, but it brought the house down.

After the show we had some drinks and then they dropped me off at the hotel where I was staying. When I unlocked my door, I flipped on the light to see Billy Connoly himself standing there playing a banjo and singing *Drivin' My Life Away*! What a shock! Terry Oates had set me up and it was a great surprise. I ended up hanging out with Billy for a couple hours that night at two or nine pubs and having a high old time.

After a few days in England we flew to Paris and stayed a couple of days. I went antiquing and took a boat excursion up the Seine River under bridges still in use that were built in the 1400's. We in America think two hundred years is a long time while they are still using bridges in Paris that are over six hundred years old.

From Paris we flew to Cannes, France where the yearly Midem Convention was taking place. It's a gathering of music publishers, record labels, managers and recording artists making deals and hobnobbing for a week. I hung out with my buddy, Ralph Murphy from Nashville, and I swear he knew everybody in France! Through Ralph's contacts I met Bill Wyman, the long time original bassist with The Rolling Stones and that was a hoot. I also met Demis Roussos, a gigantic recording artist in Europe, virtually unheard of in the United States. Ralph was partners with another good friend of mine, Roger Cook, in the publishing firm, Pic-A-Lic Music, just two doors down from our offices on Music Row. Roger hails from England and has written some of the standard classics of our time, such as The Hollies, *Long Cool Woman (In A Black Dress)* and *I'd Like To Teach The World To Sing* just to name a few. Ralph is no slouch songwriting-wise as well, with Crystal Gayle's, *Talking In Your Sleep* to his credit. During the 70's and 80's there were no hotter independent publishing companies in Music City than our two companies.

It just so happened that the aforementioned Cowboy Jack Clement was also in Cannes at the time we were there, and staying at the same hotel. The French think a loaf of white bread and some cheese is a great breakfast. We, and Jack, didn't think so. So, in the great Cowboy tradition, on the third day he marched into the hotel kitchen and took over the place, announcing that he would, from now on, be cooking breakfast for all of our American group, which he did!

It was a life-changing experience roaming through Europe, and I remember the high this small-town Ohio boy got while visiting Monte Carlo, in a casino on the French Riviera, when my attorney and friend, John Mason, got the call with the news that, *I Love A Rainy Night* had just gone number one on the American Pop Charts. What a memorable moment that was.

To put the icing on the cake, The Chipmunks recorded "Urban Chipmunk," a country album of hit songs and *I Love A Rainy Night* was included. I received a framed gold album for sales of half a million records by my new three little varmint friends.

Someday I'm Gonna Rent This Town

CHAPTER 28

....

Paul Overstreet

There were other strong songs on the "Horizon" album, like *What Will I Write*, a song I later produced on Engelbert Humperdinck for Epic Records, and *I Need To Fall In Love Again,* written by myself and a brand new writer that Jim discovered from Mississippi named Paul Overstreet. Paul was a young man but a seasoned performer who came to Nashville with big dreams of making it as a professional songwriter. He and I hit it right off, even sharing a house for a while, partying and writing up a storm.

I introduced Paul to Dr. Hook's producer, Ron Haffkine, and he ended up producing Paul's very first album for the RCA label. That scored him his first chart record, *Beautiful Baby,* a song we wrote that I later recorded and produced on Engelbert Humperdinck as well. Paul wrote many songs for our company and has remained one of my best buddies. Some of Paul's credits include: *When You Say Nothing At All* recorded and made famous by Keith Whitley as well as Alison Krauss, *Forever and Ever Amen, Diggin' Up Bones* and *On The Other Hand* by Randy Travis, *Some Beach* by Blake Shelton and *Same Old Me,* by George Jones. He also had a slew of his own big hits as a singer, such as, *Sowin' Love, Daddy's Come Around* and *Seein' My Father In Me,* as well as *A Long Line Of Love,* sung by Michael Martin Murphy. Paul holds the distinguished record of being the only songwriter named BMI Songwriter of The Year five times in a row! Paul was inducted into the Songwriter's Hall Of Fame in 2003. What a great songwriter he is.

Someday I'm Gonna Rent This Town

CHAPTER 29

....

Step by Step

The next Eddie Rabbitt album, "Step By Step," also cut at Caribou Ranch, produced three singles including the title track, which went to number one on the Country charts and reached the top 5 on both the Adult Contemporary and Billboard Top Pop 100 charts. That song was written one morning with Eddie and David in my cabin at Caribou Ranch. We went right in and recorded *Step By Step* within hours of writing it. Eddie's acoustic guitar playing on that tune is, in my opinion, one of his finest performances.

The "Step By Step" album included *Someone Could Lose a Heart Tonight* also reaching number one Country and made the top 15 on the other two charts as well. Cutting this song was unique, in that it was the first time we got the opportunity to work with Billy Joe Walker Jr., a renowned Los Angeles session guitar player. He was known for coming up with signature acoustic parts like that great riff on Juice Newton's *Queen of Hearts*. He's played on hit records by everyone from Merle Haggard and Glen Campbell to The Beach Boys. On *Someone Could Lose A Heart Tonight* he came up with that repetitive electric guitar part that runs throughout the song . . . so cool.

Eddie liked to call that song our "Halloween Valentine."

The fine song, *I Don't Know Where to Start*, written by Thom Schuyler, another undiscovered songwriter we signed to our companies, peaked at two and nine on the Country and Adult contemporary charts, respectively.

Someday I'm Gonna Rent This Town

....

CHAPTER 30

Thom Schuyler is Discovered

How we stumbled onto Thom's talents is one big stroke of luck. I'd met a carpenter in Union City, Tennessee, named George Sprague, way back when, during the construction of the recording studio I built with my uncle Bob. George and I, because we were so broke, used to pay for an all-you-can-eat smorgasbord for lunch and hang around long enough to stay for a free dinner too. He became a good friend and eventually moved to Music City. We hired him to build an addition on to our building at 16th Ave South to house a 24 track studio we came to name The Garage. George had met Thom Schuyler while building stage sets for a local theater and brought him onboard to help build our studio. We had no idea Thom was a budding songwriter until he gave a cassette tape of four or five of his songs to Keni Wehrman, our secretary at the publishing company. She was impressed and gave me the tape to listen to. I put it into my car's glove compartment and drove around with it for a few weeks. On the way to an Eddie Rabbitt mix session at Woodland Studios, I happened on it and stuck it into my player. I was amazed at the quality of the songs on that tape and came to the session ranting and raving about the songs I had just heard. My partners agreed that Thom was a superb and special songwriter and we signed him to an exclusive songwriting deal within a few days. In fact, his song, *I Don't Know Where To Start* was on that tape, recorded and included on the album we were mixing that very week.

Thom went on to write many hit songs for our organization

. . . *Old Yellow Car*, made famous by the late Dan Seals, *Years After You* by John Conlee, and the great story song about Nashville song-writers, *16th Avenue* by Lacy J. Dalton. Though I don't remember it, Thom swears to this day that he had all but discarded the half-written song, *16th Avenue*, not thinking it was a viable song, until he played it for me and I encouraged him to finish it.

Down the line Thom teamed up with Paul Overstreet and singer and songwriter Fred Knobloch, to form the trio SKO (Schuyler, Knobloch, Overstreet), releasing seven singles including the number one cut, Baby's Got A New Baby. Thom went on to become chairman of the Country Music Association and also headed RCA Records' Nashville division from 1992 to 1995, signing Lonestar, Kenny Chesney and played an important role in the careers of Martina McBride and Sara Evans. He was inducted into the Songwriter's Hall of Fame in 2011.

CHAPTER 31

Emerald Studio

David Malloy and I must have thought that we had too much money, so in 1983 we built a studio against the great advice of friends who loved us.

Even though Jimmy Carter was the President and interest rates were soaring out of this world, we built a studio, and we named it "Emerald Sound."

Well, at least we built the best damn studio in Nashville! Top of the line everything: Neve recording console, the best Studer recorders, rooms acoustically designed, a live tiled room just for recording guitar amps, Yamaha Grand Piano, Italian tiles in the bathrooms, copper sinks, video games for downtime, and a hidden room behind a secretly hinged control room wall, where we could hide when we wanted to disappear.

After we made the decision to build the studio, we found a great building. It was an ancient stone church on Music Row owned by Tony & Susan Alamo of Christian TV fame. This was a strange couple to watch on television and even stranger to buy a property from. Supposedly, Tony kept his deceased wife at home for months after her passing, planning on her eventual resurrection. We thought the church could make an incredible recording studio and spent forever trying to close the deal, but to no avail. Years later, that church was bought by Mike Curb, eventually turned into Ocean Way Studio and donated to Belmont University's Music Department.

We pressed on and found a great classic building on 17th Ave

South. It needed restoration but its bones were good. Of course you never know what you're getting into when you build a studio. We poured concrete for the main floor to be built on, but the rebar they put into the concrete for strength picked up radio signals that came through our speaker system and we had to tear it up and start over.

While excavating, we hit a six foot tall ancient sewer pipe that ran right through the center of the main room and had to remove that and completely reinforce that area.

The first construction company we hired ripped us off with exorbitant prices and workers who did nothing but screw off and steal things. We had to fire and sue them and start over, putting us way behind schedule.

Exotic tiles and other special order materials mysteriously disappeared overnight, but we built a studio!

CHAPTER 32

....

You and I

At about this time, Jim Malloy found a song written by a writer named Frank Myers. The song was *You And I*. Jim was sure this song was a hit and firmed up a deal to publish it and try to get Eddie Rabbitt to record it. Eddie thought it was a cool song but kept putting the recording of it off until the very last session, and the very last fifteen minutes of that session for the album, "Radio Romance." He did record it though and as soon as it was in the can, it was decided to make it into a duet with some super female artist. Dolly Parton first came to mind, but she had already been doing many duets with Kenny Rogers and felt that it would be strange to do another with someone else. Then Olivia Newton John came up as a possibility, but she was not available. Then the perfect voice for the song came along . . . Crystal Gayle.

Our studio, Emerald Sound, was almost completed . . . just some walls and cosmetic touches here and there and we would be in business. The recording equipment was in place and working like a charm, so David decided to overdub Crystal's vocal at Emerald Sound. They covered the studs of the vocal booth with plastic and blankets and Crystal did a beautiful performance, although the real magic happened as she was learning the melody. David and Crystal sat in the control room listening to the cut of *You And I* with Eddie's vocal already on it and as each phrase of the verse passed, Crystal would repeat the line after him, learning the melody that way. David had a brain storm . . . that's how she should do the verses, echoing each of Eddie's lines. It was a brilliant idea and made the record unique and a favorite song sung at people's weddings to this day. You should have seen the look on Frank Myer's face when Jim handed him his first royalty check, which I believe was for $60,000!

We hired a girl whose job was to keep the studio booked. She would tell us each month that we were totally booked solid, then at the last minute, inform us that a major artist had to cancel. We always seemed to end up with unbooked days each week. Of course, we allowed major artists the luxury of cancellations, because we didn't want to lose their business. But after a year of this we discovered our employee was lying to us all along, telling us she had the studio booked by big artists, when it wasn't. It was her clever ploy to make herself look good and to keep her job. It was our own fault . . . we were off doing other projects and not around every day to keep tabs on things. Through it all we won Studio of the Year many years in a row and were very proud of our accomplishment.

During the years we owned Emerald Sound, we had the cream of the crop making records there, including The Highwaymen, Willie Nelson, Kris Kristofferson, Waylon Jennings & Johnny Cash. Producer Jimmy Bowen booked our studio solidly with acts like Hank Williams Jr, Reba McIntire, Glen Campbell, Kenny Rogers, The Oak Ridge Boys, George Strait, Suzy Bogguss and Kim Carnes. David Malloy brought in acts to produce such as Rosanne Cash and J.D. Souther. I produced Hillary Kanter for the RCA Label and the very first full album recorded there on international superstar, Engelbert Humperdinck. In 1986 we sold Emerald Sound to a man from Montana and it remained a top studio in Nashville, still winning awards year after year.

CHAPTER 33

....

Till You and Your Lover are Lovers Again

Five years after the infamous tape-eating fiasco of *When You're In Love With A Beautiful Woman*, Engelbert called me one day, out of the blue. He had just finished recording an album with producer Mike Post in Los Angeles for Epic Records and wanted me to send or write him a big hit to include on the album. I began by sending him five songs that I really believed in and I thought would give him what he was after. After receiving the tape he called me to say he loved every one of the songs and asked if I would be interested in producing a whole new album on him! I asked him what Epic records would think of that and he said, "No problem, I will pay for it all myself, that's how confident I am that we will make a killer album."

I called up all the top songwriters I knew and asked them for their best songs to send to Engelbert. They gave me some super tunes that he loved and wanted to record. When we had an album's worth of songs in hand, I checked the progress of Emerald and it's opening date and booked the sessions to begin that day. I hand-picked the primo players: James Stroud & Owen Hale on Drums, Billy Joe Walker Jr on Acoustic & Electric Guitars, Dan Huff on Acoustic & Electric Guitar, Spadey Brannan on Bass, Randy McCormick on Keyboards and Larry Byrom on Electric Guitar & Piano. I hired the great Joe Bogan as Chief Engineer, famous for engineering many hits by Seals & Crofts.

What a ball we had making that album! Listening to that

golden voice of Engelbert's every day was a thrill every producer should experience . . . that man can SING! On top of that, he was fun to be around, work with, and all the Nashville players liked him and gave their very best. As a unexpected bonus, Engelbert asked the great Marilyn McCoo to duet with him on a song I wrote with Steve Davis called *Two Lovers*. The first single released off the album was the title song, *Till You And Your Lover*, a song written by Jan Buckingham and Mark Gray. It charted at 17 Adult Contemporary, top thirty Country and lingered in the Hot 100 Pop in the 70's.

During the recording of the "Till You and Your Lover" album, the BMI Songwriter's Awards were coming up and I asked Engelbert if he would like to attend as my guest. He balked at that, thinking that he wouldn't be welcomed since he wasn't a songwriter. I assured him he would have a great time and people would love seeing him there. When Engelbert walked into that ballroom you could see the women melt in their chairs. I was amazed at the reaction to him and the charisma that he had. With that voice and that charisma I clearly understood his worldwide fame.

At Emerald Studio with Engelbert.

CHAPTER 34

You Can't Run from Love

The second single from Eddie Rabbitt's Radio Romance album was *You Can't Run From Love*. I remember sitting around the kitchen table at our publishing company making up this song with Eddie and David Malloy. I particularly love the bridge of this song. *"You can travel in a time machine, disappear without a trace, But it don't matter where you go, It'll find you anyplace. You can't run from love."* Short and sweet, that's the way I like 'em. I recall us having a struggle getting the label to promote this record. The label head had just changed and Jimmy Bowen was now in charge and seemed skeptical about our tune. Despite the troubles it still had the legs to be a summertime hit. Number one Country, Number one in adult Contemporary, as well as a number one in Canada and a mid-chart Hot 100 Pop record too.

Rewind:

While working on the Radio Romance album at Village Recorders in Los Angeles with David and Eddie, another gift from above came my way.

Village Recorders was a very hip place to make music. Fleetwood Mac recorded the "Rumours" album there, which became 1978's Album of the Year, eventually selling over 40 million copies. In a very smart move, the owner of the studio, Gordie Hormel, had the good sense to build Fleetwood Mac their own beautiful state of the art recording studio in the back of the complex.

I was thrilled to be working in the same building in one of their other two studios, breathing the same air as one of my favorite singers, Stevie Nicks.

Taking a break one night, I was standing in the front entrance, when in walked three gorgeous women of the black persuasion. I purchased a new pair of shoes that afternoon at Fred Segal's famous store on Melrose Avenue. One of the girls looked at them and said, "Them are some cool Stomps!" After a little chit-chat they asked me if I wanted to come back to the studio where they were working as background singers, and I said, "Sure, I'd love too." There was a party going on in their studio, with four or five session players cranking it up, two recording engineers at the board, and a half dozen or so people in the control room just grooving to the music. I was the only white person in the room, but nobody seemed to notice or care. I was curious which artist would be recording that night, then he walked in . . . Marvin Gaye. I'm talking about the guy who sang *How Sweet It Is (To Be Loved By You), I Heard It Through The Grapevine, It Takes Two Baby* and co-wrote *Beechwood 4-5789*! Hell, he sang the soundtrack to my young life. I was in hog heaven.

I discovered something that night about recording that I carry with me to every session I've had since then. Recording should be a joyous event. They didn't even turn on the 24 track recorder until everyone was dancing and in a good mood. There is an old saying, "Every vibe in the room goes on tape." So, I always remember, be careful who you let into the room.

Thank goodness those ladies liked my "stomps," 'cause, they were so warm and friendly and Marvin Gaye let me hang in there for hours and now I have one of the most treasured memories of my professional life.

CHAPTER 35

Love Will Turn You Around

One fateful Thursday night a call came in from Kenny Roger's office.

Kenny had just wrapped up shooting a film about car racing starring himself and a new actress, Diane Lane. Kenny was positive that she was destined to become a huge star and he was looking for a hit song to be the theme song for his movie, "Six Pack." He asked if we were interested in writing him one. We said, "No, will you quit bothering us!"

NOT REALLY . . . We said, "Of course we will!"

Kenny Rogers was about as hot as any artist could possibly be at the time, just coming off of successes like *Lady* and *Through the Years*. David and I were hot-to-trot to come through for him. He was scheduled to give a concert in Lexington, Kentucky that weekend and suggested that we come up and meet with him before the concert and discuss the project. David said to me, "Let's drive up on Saturday morning . . . " I interrupted saying, "What we need to do is rent a big shiny Silver Eagle tour bus, with a driver, put our songwriting gear on there and carve out a song for Kenny on the way up to Lexington."

That's exactly what we did. On the trip we started a song about racing and had about half of it done by the time we arrived backstage at the colosseum where Kenny was about to perform. His people escorted us to his dressing room, we said our hello's and told him we had a song started for him. I took out my guitar and began singing our half-written song, but I could feel the flop sweat setting in on me as I realized that our tune sucked and I still had more to sing. Just then Kenny saved me by cutting in with "No, I don't want a song about racing in particular, just one that ties in to the movie somehow and is an out-and-out smash radio song. Look, I have to go on stage now, here's a little guitar thing I like." He played an infectious, two-note back and forth guitar lick, sang a catchy simple melody and said, "Take that and see what you might be able to do with it! I have front row seats for you guys. I hope you enjoy the show."

Kenny Rogers put on one hell of a show that night but it seemed like he sang 500 songs, because between every song, I would have to turn to David or he'd have to turn to me, and sing the melody that Kenny had briefly shown us. When we got back on the bus and headed home we started writing our new song and decided we should bring Thom Schuyler in on it. We stopped at a truck stop in the middle of the night and called Thom and told him, "If you are any kind of a songwriter, you will meet us when we pull in to the office and write this song for Kenny with us." Thom came through, and by the next afternoon we had the song *Love Will Turn You Around* all written. We booked Ray Stevens's Sound Lab studio and brought in our buddies, Randy McCormick on keyboards, Billy Joe Walker Jr on guitars, and Spady Brannon on Bass and demoed the song with Thom singing the lead vocal. We overnighted the song to Kenny and he got right back to us saying, "I love it . . . fly on out here and we'll make a record!"

David and I arrived in Los Angeles the next day, checked into the L'Ermitage Hotel, rented a car and drove to Kenny's Lion Share Studios to record. When we got there Kenny had all seven people in his road band set up to record in a small studio. David and I looked at each other in shock as Kenny said, "I've always promised someday to make a record with my road band, so here we go."

No aspersions on road bands, but we were used to cutting records with a very small select group of studio musicians, so this setup made us very nervous. We tried all day to cut *Love Will Turn*

You Around, but it just wasn't coming out to our liking. To add more confusion to the mix, Kenny had three studios in his complex at Lion Share and had monster producer, David Foster, with him in one studio making a record, and superstar Lionel Richie in another, producing him. Kenny would make his rounds between all three projects.

At the end of day one, David took Kenny aside and told him that the recording wasn't working out. Kenny was cool about it and said, "Okay, hire whoever you'd like and we'll try again." So the "A" session players in Los Angeles were booked for day two. We recorded the whole day and still it didn't quite sound right. We realized that our demo, built around a drum machine groove, Randy McCormick's piano and Billy Joe Walker's amazing acoustic guitar was perfect, but unfortunately, in the wrong key for Kenny to sing to.

We had our staff in Nashville overnight our drum machine to us, flew Billy Joe and Randy McCormick out on the red eye flight and the next day we finally we got that track sounding magical! Drummer, Paul Liem came in and overdubbed some awesome percussion and David Hungate laid down perfection for a bass line. During the recording process Kenny had doubts that our verses were written as well as they should've been and I spent many hours on the phone with Thom Schuyler, back in Nashville, rewriting lyrics to run by Kenny. When Kenny wasn't available, I had the job of singing his part when we were trying out the new lyrics. When it was time for him to sing the master, Kenny asked me what lyrics I thought were the right ones and I told him honestly that I thought the original lyrics were always right. He said, "Great, let's go with them!" Then he went out to the mic and sang his ass off.

A funny note to that whole experience: After all the musicians had gone home, Kenny wanted to have someone put a piano "E" note on the downbeats throughout most of the song, so I went out to the Rhodes piano and played that one note all through the record. I got paid by the musician's union for my efforts and when I got back home to Nashville I found that I was listed in the musician's union book as a keyboardist. For the next few months I would get telephone calls to book me on sessions as a keyboard player and I always had to ask, "What note do you want me to play? They would always be puzzled and I would tell them, "I only do "E" notes!"

Love Will Turn You Around went up the charts like a rocket and garnered Kenny and us a tub full of awards:

- Grammy Nomination: Best Country Vocal Performance
- Academy of Country Music Nomination: Single Record of the Year
- Academy of Country Music Nomination: Album of the year
- American Music Awards: Favorite Country Single
- American Music Awards: Favorite Country Vocal

It was a number one record Country as well as Adult Contemporary, and reached number 13 on the Hot 100 Pop Charts. It also went number one in Canada and reached 3 Million airplay status with BMI. On the many award shows, Kenny was always so gracious and went out of his way to thank us profusely, and as I said, "Kenny sang his ass off!"

Rewind:

I spent a week one night with Roger Miller.

I got a phone call from the head of BMI, my friend and supporter, Francis Preston, saying, "Even, I think you should meet Roger Miller."

Roger and his wife, Mary Arnold, former singer with Kenny Rogers and The First Edition, were staying at the Spence Manor Hotel on Music Row, located right across the street from BMI's headquarters. I showed up that evening and Roger and I jived-up immediately and began elevating our mood. He told me about just recently meeting a Broadway producer who encouraged him to write a stage play called Big River and he was in the process of writing the songs for that project. He played me song after song, including *Dadgum Gov'ment, I, Huckleberry, Me* and *River In The Rain*. He wanted to know if I thought they were good enough, and I honestly said, "They sure sound great to me . . . but what the hell do I know about Broadway?" It won an arms full of Tony Awards for Roger.

That night, we started swapping songs and I played him a funny song called *Key West Skies*, all about a guy who picks up a girl, takes her to bed, and discovers it's really a guy in drag. Roger thought it was incredible and told me he was going to cut it on sessions he was getting ready to do with Harold Shedd, the legendary record producer for the group, Alabama. They created a great record and wanted to release it but Roger's label was scared shitless of it. Later that year, he told me that he used *Key West Skies* on stage as his encore number and that it always brought the house down. I sure was proud of that cut, not only because Roger was such a great artist and songwriter, but that he seldom recorded songs that he didn't write. Looking back at that night, I remember his wife, Mary, sticking her head out of the bedroom door every hour or so saying, "Are you still here?" Roger and I just smiled and kept on playing until dawn.

Someday I'm Gonna Rent This Town

CHAPTER 36

....

Big Changes Afoot

1984 became a year of big changes for "the trinity." David decided that he was no longer interested in producing records on Eddie Rabbitt and they parted ways professionally.

Undaunted, Eddie and I began writing songs for a new album. It was strange, but it was like old times again, just he and I sitting in a room making it all happen. I suggested that he name the new album *The Best Year of My Life* and concentrate on positive upbeat songs. Eddie thought that was a great idea and a great title for a song. So we sat down to write it, which we did. Our song, *The Best Year Of My Life* climbed to number one in the USA and Canada.

Rewind:

While working at Emerald Sound on the song, *The Best Year Of My Life*, my mother, Opal, and my grandmother, Sally McGee, were in town and came by to listen to us record some high background harmonies. If you ever sat in on an overdub session, you'd find that the producer and engineer tend to play one section of the song, "ad nauseam," until they get the recording just right. The casual observer, bless their heart, can't help but find it boring. When I got the part exactly how I wanted it, I asked my grandmother what she thought of the tune. She said, in her honest, Kentucky hills sort of way, "If I never hear that song again, it'll be too soon!"

For this album, Eddie and I had an urge to get back to our rockabilly roots and wrote a thumper called *Warning Sign*. We jammed-up one night in our studio, The Garage, and I programmed some drums on a new piece of gear called, the Emulater. Eddie laid down a smoking acoustic track and vocal, we called in our buddy Larry Byrom on electric guitar and Spady Brannon on bass, and that sucker was soup! Nobody was better at stacking harmonies than Eddie, and I relished running the board and getting them nice and tight with him. We loved that demo, all about falling in love with someone you know is "trouble." We played *Warning Sign* 'till we wore it out.

While driving into town one night to meet up for another writing session with Eddie, I passed the Nashville airport as this plane came in for a landing, so low over my car I could see a woman's face in one of the little round windows. You never know when a song idea will hit you and for some reason I thought, *She's Coming Back To Say Goodbye*. I couldn't wait to get to our office to write that idea. Ed jumped all over it and we knocked that one out in no time and went in and demoed it that very night.

Also that night, in a quirky mood, we wrote, *Go To Sleep Big Bertha*. While discussing the greats of rockabilly, we thought it would be a hoot to write an answer to the Everly Brothers' song, *Wake Up Little Susie*, the Felice and Boudleau Bryant-written classic. One of my favorite lines we came up with was, *"I was short and fat when I met her, Now I'm tall and lean....Good God, Stop, don't get on top, It'll be the last you ever see of me! Go to sleep Big Bertha!"* Great fun . . . Hey, sometimes ya just gotta get a little crazy.

Billy Joe Walker Jr. was crashing on my couch at the time, and we were writing quite a few songs together. I asked Eddie if he wanted to write one with Billy and we three came up with another rockabilly tune titled, *B-B-B-Burnin' Up With Love*. Built around Billy's unbelievable guitar playing, we carved out something we thought was very unique, a lyric about a girl so hot that she makes a man stutter. We laughingly joked that it would be a perfect song for M-M-Mel Tillis. Well, I guess the joke was on us because it went straight to number one, and man, it sounded so good on the radio.

Eddie and I were set to produce his new album along with

Signed CD from Martina.

*Me and my great friend
Jerry McLaughlin.*

Me and Eddie in the early days.

BMI's Frances Preston and I at the BMI Awards.

Seth at the helm.

Top row: Jody Williams of BMI, Jim Malloy, Thom Schuyler and David Preston of BMI. Front row: David Malloy, Janine Rabbitt and Even Stevens

Jimmy Bowen, the head honcho at Warner Brothers Records, now Eddie's new label. Session players were booked and we recorded for two or three days. Two songs we believed were a couple of our best and most likely singles just didn't come off right to us on playback. We talked with Jimmy and told him we wanted to put out our demos of the songs instead because they were better than the session tracks. He wasn't exactly thrilled about it, but agreed. Luckily I was set up with an engineer that I really liked for the overdubs and vocal work that I took on as producer. Dave Hassinger was the engineer and he had worked on many records that I loved, including albums by The Rolling Stones, Jefferson Airplane, Love, Crosby Stills Nash and Young, the Grateful Dead, The Jackson 5, Leo Kotke, Seals and Crofts and George Strait. He was a good dude and really knew his stuff and I was honored to work with him. He helped mix up our two demoes of *Warning Sign* and *B-B-B-Burnin' Up With Love*. The next release that summer was the album title song, *The Best Year of My Life*. We were flying high, not aware of what trouble waited right around the bend in 1985.

Me & Billy Joe.

Someday I'm Gonna Rent This Town

CHAPTER 37

Real Life Steps In

Eddie and his wife Janine's second child was a beautiful son named Timmy who was diagnosed with biliary atresia at birth. The condition required a liver transplant for his very survival, and he underwent the transplant in the summer of 1985. Sadly the attempt failed and Timmy passed away. It was a very hard time for Eddie, Janine, and their daughter Demelza, and it put Eddie's recording and touring career on hold for quite some time.

Warner Bros. had already released the single, *Warning Sign*, in the spring of 1985 and it did well, reaching number four and number three in both the US and Canada respectively. Eddie wanted to slow things down and spend time with his family so he curtailed his personal appearances, both on television and on tour. The fourth single, *She's Coming Back to Say Goodbye*, was released in the fall. It reached number three on the R&R charts and number six in Billboard. 1985 was very successful record wise, but for my buddy Ed, it certainly was not the best year of his life.

Someday I'm Gonna Rent This Town

....

CHAPTER 38

Selling Our Publishing Company to Mary Tyler Moore/MTM

For the first time in my songwriting career, during the winter of 1985 and the spring of 1986, I was not sequestered away with Eddie Rabbitt. That was the time in past years when he came off the road and we buckled down to write twenty or thirty songs from which to choose the best of the lot for a new album.

As it turned out, writing a killer next album with Eddie would have been difficult at best because some of the partners in the publishing companies decided that they wanted to make some serious career moves.

David and his wife Shari made the decision to move to Los Angeles. Dave wanted to try his hand at becoming a full-fledged pop producer. Jim Malloy was ready to sell and retire and Eddie was willing to agree to the sale as well. I saw this as an opportunity to buy my partners out and began negotiations with Jim to do just that. I had great faith that there were some fantastic songs in our extensive catalog that could still be exploited and would be a great investment.

Getting that deal solidified proved to be a hard thing to do. Jim and I would talk and negotiate a sell price for his and David's share of the companies, but when the figures were placed before the attorney that was hired to sell our companies, he advised Jim against selling to me. This happened over and over, and as time moved on I became more obsessed with trying to close the deal and it was wearing me out. It appeared to me that the only reason we couldn't close the deal for me to purchase the shares of the other partner's came down to the fact that the attorney in charge would make considerably less money from the sale if it was sold to me. He was working on a percentage basis and when my share was subtracted from the overall sale price, he stood to make less. I was racking up attorney fees myself in negotiations for the sale and my time was being spent in a nonproductive way for months, not writing songs, unhappy, and perturbed with they way things were going. Finally I gave up and the companies were sold to Mary Tyler Moore, the MTM corporation. I had my misgivings about that company ever doing anything other than sit on the income stream already in place and it proved out that way. I can't recall ever having one song recorded out of our catalog in the years after MTM bought it.

Our catalog was eventually resold to the BNA organization and then they sold it to EMI Music Publishing where it stayed until it recently was absorbed by Sony/ATV Music. I bought the two Music Row buildings and The Garage Recording studio from my partners and formed a new publishing company called ESP Music.

CHAPTER 39

....

New Producers

Eddie signed a new deal with RCA Records and they wanted him to record with legendary producer Phil Ramone, known for his work with Billy Joel, Julian Lennon, and many other pop acts. Eddie traveled to New York City and recorded an entire album, including one song that Eddie and I had written called *A World Without Love*. That song was the only single released from that endeavor and a source of exasperation for me. Phil Ramone arranged for another writer to compose a bridge section to our song, without my knowledge or permission, and that writer became a co-writer on the song with Eddie and I. I wasn't very happy. The song didn't need a make-it-or-break-it bridge, and if it did, Eddie and I should have handled it. The single peaked at number 10 and the album was shelved by RCA, who then turned him over to another producer, Richard Landis. I don't know what it was about bridges all of a sudden, but even he wanted one third of the rights to a song we wrote, simply for suggesting we add a bridge. Although Eddie insisted I be at all of his recording sessions, especially his vocal sessions, Mr. Landis wasn't particularly cordial towards me, and we didn't exactly hit it off. Those efforts produced the album "Rabbitt Trax," with the singles, *Gotta Have You*, *Repetitive Regret*, and a duet with Juice Newton called *Both To Each Other*, which went number one in 1986. The Phil Ramone produced single ended up on the Rabbitt Trax album as well.

Eddie's decision to take the label's advice when it came to the creative part of his songwriting and recording career began to cause us to drift apart as songwriting partners. The writing became more of a job to write a chart hit rather than just letting it flow, which had always been our method of writing in the past. I became busy writing for and producing other projects, but it was painful to watch it all go down, so I slowly eased out of the situation and went through a blue period, feeling the loss of our great partnership.

CHAPTER 40

Hillary Kanter

During all of this craziness, I flew up to the Big Apple for the BMI Pop Awards and met a young woman songwriter named Hillary Kanter at the baggage claim in the John F. Kennedy Airport. She was moving to Nashville and we began cooperating and getting our songs on records by Dolly Parton, Lacy J. Dalton, The Oak Ridge Boys, Conway Twitty, and many others. Prior to our meeting, she sang on stage with international star Julio Iglesias in concerts throughout Europe.

Hillary possessed a beautiful voice and I recorded a few songs on her, and RCA Records signed her to their roster in 1984. She had two albums on RCA, and three singles charted and won her an Academy of Country Music/ACM nomination in 1985 for "Best New Female Country Artist." Her second album was titled after my song, *Crazy In Love*, a song co-written with keyboard great, Randy McCormick. I was convinced that this was a number one release for Hillary, but try as we may, we could not get the label to release it as a single. They felt that the only way to break a new artist was with an up tempo song and not a ballad. We never did get that recording of hers on the airwaves.

Hillary eventually decided to leave RCA and after a short stint with the MCA label, she returned to songwriting full-time. Over the next few years she had her songs recorded by Tim Mc-Graw with *Carry On*, Ricky Skaggs with *Lovin' Only Me*, Barbara Mandrell singing *I'll Leave Something Good Behind,* and Martina

McBride with *A Great Disguise.* Currently she is concentrating on writing very unique books, including such jewels as "Dating Sucks" and "Dead Men Are Easy To Love."

CHAPTER 41

Joe Cocker

Shortly after Hillary's version of *Crazy In Love* was recorded for the country market, Joe Cocker cut my song, which was included on his "Civilized Man" album. I was invited to the sessions, produced by Stewart Levine, who had produced that wonderful record, *Up Where We Belong* on Joe and Jennifer Warnes. He had produced other classic hits like *If You Don't Know Me By Now* by Simply Red and albums by a who's who of talent. He was recording Joe in Nashville, across the street from my office at David Briggs' cool studio. When they cut *Crazy In Love* it was spectacular sounding, and Joe Cocker's vocal was stark and emotional in the fashion of *You Are So Beautiful To Me*, one of his other monster hits. I was so pumped when I left that session. To me, a recording of a song by Joe Cocker was the pinnacle of songwriting success. He was my favorite ever since my hippie days in San Francisco when I went to see him and Leon Russell "live" in The Mad Dogs and Englishman Tour at the Fillmore.

Months passed before the album was released, and in the meantime another producer was brought in to produce Joe and, in the process he took Stewart's work on *Crazy In Love*, reworked, re-recorded the vocal, and it became a pale reflection of the magic I had heard at the session.

In 1988 *Crazy In Love* became a single and an Adult Contemporary hit for the smoky-voiced, Kim Carnes. She recorded a sparse soulful version of my song on the MCA label and it was beautiful, reaching the number 12 position.

Rewind:

During this time I bought a house on Old Hickory Lake. Jim Malloy married Dolly's sister, Stella Parton, and they lived on a bucolic hidden cove not far from a popular sailboating harbor. When the house next door came up for sale, Jim suggested that I buy it, so I did and spent much of my time boating, fishing, and goofing off around the pool. Jim and Stella eventually got divorced and Dolly bought the house and used it as a getaway. On a television show one night the host asked her why she liked being secluded on the lake and she replied in her beloved, Smoky Mountain way, "You know, sometimes I just like to pee off the porch!" You wouldn't believe the hours I wasted trying to catch a glimpse of that!

CHAPTER 42

Dolly Parton and Tina Turner

Eddie Rabbitt was invited to guest on the TNN television show, "Dolly" starring who else but, Dolly Parton. I tagged along and during a break on the set I found myself lucky enough to be sitting at a small cafe table with two of the sexiest women in the world . . . Dolly Parton and Tina Turner! Tina had yet to make her big come-back with the song, *What's Love Got To Do With It*, and during our conversation she put her hand on my shoulder and said, "Why don't you write *me* one of those big hit songs?" I guess I was in such a daze and confused state from the sheer pulchritude surrounding me that I couldn't say what I should've said, which was, "Oh my God, I would love to write you a song, you goddess, you!" No, my numb mind was thinking, "She hasn't had a hit for a while, hhmmm, maybe I should get her phone number . . . Naw!" Eddie and I had a saying for that kind of stupid thinking by a song writer, "Oh, too rich to write, ehh?"

Dear Tina, if by some stretch of the imagination, you are reading this, I apologize and regret it every day that I didn't take you up on your wonderful request . . . you are the Rock and Roll QUEEN.

Someday I'm Gonna Rent This Town

....

CHAPTER 43

Lovin' Only Me

In 1989 Hillary and I wrote an up tempo song called *Lovin' Only Me*.

Ricky Skaggs had put out the word on Music Row that he was going to produce an album on Dolly Parton and was looking for hits. She had recorded some other songs of ours earlier, so I thought *Lovin' Only Me* was a natural for her. Ricky wanted songwriters and publishers to drop off tapes of potential songs for Dolly at his office, which was just down the road from mine, but I had no faith in pitching songs in that manner. I've sat in front of producers and A&R people at labels enough to know that there are usually hundreds of tapes or CD's stacked on their desks that don't stand an ice cube's chance in hell of ever being heard! So I bugged Ricky, over a period of weeks to please come down to my studio and listen to this one song. Finally, he called and said he would be over.

He loved the song and put it on hold to play for Dolly. A few days later he called and told me that Dolly thought the song was a hit but that it sounded more like a man's song. We were disappointed because who doesn't want a Dolly Parton cut? Ricky then asked, "Would you mind letting me cut it for my next album?" Well, that was a wonderful surprise and we eagerly gave him the song. He and Steve Buckingham produced a great record and Ricky brought in the English guitar wizard, Albert Lee, whom Ricky had known from their days working in Emmy Lou Harris's Hot Band, to play his flashy style of lead guitar. Albert Lee's credits are a mile long. He

Left to Right: CBS's Roy Wunch, co-writer Hillary Kanter, Ricky Skaggs, me and producer Steve Buckingham

worked with the Everly Brothers for twenty odd years, and with Eric Clapton for about five. He played such a funky guitar part on *Lovin' Only Me*. Our song became Ricky Skaggs' twelfth number one and his last number one as of this writing . . . but you should never write off Ricky.

CHAPTER 44

No Matter How High

In 1990 the charts belonged to Garth Brooks, but I managed to slide in three major successes during his years. The first thing that came along, The Oak Ridge Boys recorded a song that I wrote with Joey Scarbury.

I met Joey through David Malloy's use of his talents on background vocals. In 1981, as an artist, Joey had a huge Pop radio hit, *The Greatest American Hero Theme (Believe It Or Not)*. I started hiring him to sing some demos for me. Joey was a master of harmonies. If you wanted it to sound like The Beatles or The Beach Boys or a Bluegrass group, Joey knew the particular harmony structure to use in each case, and he had a great set of pipes.

One day, while he was hanging around the studio, I played him an idea I had and we wrote, *No Matter How High*. Joey sang the demo. It only sat on the shelf for a month or two and then the Oaks heard it, cut it, and put it out. It was a fast mover, going to the Number One spot and staying on the charts for fifteen weeks. It was so nice having a big hit with the group that so graciously sang on my own album years ago. BMI threw a super number one party for us and the Oak Ridge Boys hoisted us up on their shoulders for a photo I will always cherish. They're a good bunch of guys.

Rewind:

My father, Floyd, was responsible for my relationship with the Oak Ridge Boys. As I mentioned earlier, my father and sister

Sandy ran The Victory Institute, and distributed Bible lessons and courses on Christian music to inmates, and Duane Allen of the Oaks contributed money and time to the project. My father contacted the Grand Ole Opry and arranged to present Duane with a plaque commemorating his contributions to the cause on the Opry one Saturday night. That week Duane asked my dad if he wanted to come out to the Oak's studio in Hendersonville, Tennessee to watch him produced a young contemporary Christian band from Georgia. My dad invited me to go with him and I was excited to meet Duane.

We sat at the sound board with Duane and the engineer while they tried to record a song called *Jesus Is Coming* with the group. After about twelve takes, due mainly to the fact that the drummer thought he was on stage and was theatrically throwing his sticks in the air and usually dropping them during the recordings. Duane turned to us and said, "Jesus will be here by the time we get this one down!"

No Matter How High had barely eased off the charts when Lacy J. Dalton put out her rendition of *Black Coffee* on Capitol Records.

Left to Right: Duane Allen, Joey Scarbury, Joe Bonsall, Richard Sturben, myself and Steve Sanders.

CHAPTER 45

Black Coffee

One day I was driving to the grocery with my fourteen year old son, Seth, when he up and asked, "Hey Dad, how do you go about writing a song anyway?" I had a cup of coffee in my hand and said, "Well, you know, you can write a song about anything . . . like this cup of coffee. You could say, *"Black Coffee, Blue Mornin', Toast is burnin' and the rains keep pourin', Bad feelin', I'm losin' you.* Then you just take it from there." He nodded his head like he understood and we pulled into Kroger's parking lot and went inside.

I couldn't get that line out of my head as we walked around shopping and thinking "Hey, that was pretty frickin' good!" and by the time we left I had the song laid out in my mind. That afternoon I ran into Hillary Kanter at my office and we sat in the kitchen and carved on the idea for an hour or two and made that sucker clean! Brent Rowan, Tom Rob and Lonnie Wilson played their butts off on the stark demo sung by Hillary, and Lacy made a super record. I had to fight with the head of Capitol Records at the time to get them to produce a video on the song. He kept saying, "Videos don't help make a hit," and my answer was "Yea, right. Ask Madonna about that!" He came through though, and had a basic video made. Not only did we have a great hit with Lacy, but it began our lovely friendship that still lives to this day.

Lacy's one of the good people in this world, a true animal lover. She feeds a herd of wild mustangs every morning at her ranch in the hills of Virginia City, Nevada and fights tooth and nail for all the wild mustang's survival with her "Let 'em Run Foundation". A straight-shooter and a fine friend to have . . . and what a unique voice . . . you'd know it anywhere.

While recording *Black Coffee* at the Sound Stage studio, I also got the honor of working one day with the superb musician and artist, Glen Campbell. He and Lacy recorded a duet on *Shaky Ground*, a tune that Lacy, Hillary Kanter, and I wrote especially for the album, "Lacy J." Glen came in one afternoon, played electric guitar in a style only he can play, and performed a great vocal on our song . . . a big thrill for me. Later that week I hung around while rock & roll pioneer Carl Perkins visited Lacy, and put some hot licks on her album as well. Both Glen and Carl were so professional, friendly, and cooperative. It was a memorable week for sure, if only to get to record with Lacy J., bassist supreme Leland Sklar, guitarists Billy Joe Walker Jr. & Brent Rowan, and the keyboard coolness of John Hobbs.

....

CHAPTER 46

Conway Twitty

During the months that *Black Coffee* was having its run, they put out word at MCA Records that Conway Twitty was looking for material. At that point in my songwriting career I had previously played songs personally for Conway, but never lucked out on a cut. I will say those pitch sessions were always interesting though, and he was always such a gentleman and very musically wise. It always surprised me that he needed songs from anyone. During his early career he wrote, *It's Only Make Believe, Hello Darlin, Linda On My Mind* and *You've Never Been This Far Before*, just to name a few. But he told me he "just didn't have it in him anymore." Thank goodness, or he would have never been knighted with the Music Row praise, "Conway's the best friend a songwriter ever had." It was true, he loved songs. At his memorial I attended, Harold Reid, the bass singer for the Statler Brothers, said, "Conway was the kind of guy who, after you left the room, he'd say something nice about you."

Conway first heard *Crazy In Love* from the record I produced with Hillary Kanter on RCA, and he often said that he learned the song from her version. Produced by Jimmy Bowen, Conway, and Dee Henry, *Crazy In Love* stood out on the airwaves for it's simplicity and honest delivery, and stayed up there at number two for two weeks. His record was hot, but as I mentioned, Garth Brooks owned the charts, and *Friends In Low Places* held on to the number one for four weeks, and kept us out of that slot.

I believe that the black and white video Conway made on

Crazy In Love is the only video he ever made. He told me once that he never did videos because he felt that every listener had their own personal vision of the song in their minds from what the lyrics said to them. He didn't want to mess with that.

The following February of 1991, Kenny Rogers released *his* version of *Crazy In Love* and it peaked at number five in the Adult Contemporary charts, giving me my second hit with the iconic singer. I was told that his good friend, Kim Carnes, sang the song at his wedding and that's what gave him the idea of recording it.

That song has been a gem for me. Besides the cuts by Hillary, Joe Cocker, Kim Carnes, Conway, and Kenny Rogers, it has also been on albums by Julio Iglesias and other artists, and is to date probably my most recorded song.

CHAPTER 47

....

Meanwhile, Back at the Publishing Company

We had a talented house engineer at the Garage Studio for quite a few years named Rocky Schnaars. Rocky would rent our studio to outside clients when we were out of town. One night he had a young man booked in to sing his vocal, and he just could not get it right. Finally the guy asked Rocky to turn off all the lights in the big room he was singing in so that he could "get into it more." Rocky turn them all off, but about two minutes into the song, he detected something in the sound that he didn't like. He suddenly stopped the tape machine, threw on all the lights, and there stood the singer at the microphone . . . totally buck naked.

Someday I'm Gonna Rent This Town

CHAPTER 48

Martina McBride

In the mid 90's I decided it was time for a change. It seemed that every day there was a bucket full of problems I had to deal with to keep the publishing company running. I was tired of having a staff of people on payroll and wanted to get back to the basics and just write songs.

I also decided to quit producing records as well. Even though I enjoyed producing and working with recording artists, I didn't exactly savor the process that began after the music left the recording studio. Dealing with the labels, committees, unfulfilled promises, outright lies, luck of the draw, and general bullshit took much of the satisfaction and joy out of the effort.

I had two office buildings and a recording studio on Music Row at this time and put them on the market, selling them to producer Christie DeNapoli and promotion man Scott Brocheta, the man who later started Big Machine Records and helped make Taylor Swift an international star. My songwriting friend, Harlan Howard, offered to rent me the second floor of his beautiful stone building in Hillsboro Village and I settled in to the simpler life of a songwriter.

After moving my scaled-down operation to Harlan's building, we scored a wonderful recording on Martina McBride's super album, "Wild Angels." Co-written with Greg Barnhill, one of the writers of the Trisha Yearwood classic, *Walkaway Joe*, and my long-time cohort, Hillary Kanter, our song, *A Great Disguise*, was a great surprise. Producers Paul Worley, Martina, and Ed Seay did a spectacular job, and Paul Worley played some hot lead guitar on the cut as well. That album became a certified platinum album, selling over a million copies.

Rewind:

A few months before I sold my buildings on Music Row, I leased out one of them to a publishing company called Great Cumberland Music. The fellow who ran their day to day business was Lamar Fike, a big mountain of a guy who for years was Elvis Presley's right-hand man. Coincidentally, he was the man who helped run Hill and Range Publishing, Eddie Rabbitt's first home as a songwriter. Eddie was still writing for that company when I met him, and our first number one song, *Drinkin' My Baby (Off Of My Mind)*, was published by Hill and Range, representing Eddie's part of that song. I believe that Elvis was partnered in that company as well.

Eddie had a recording contract in the works with Columbia Records based on recording a song he had co-written with Dick Heard titled *Kentucky Rain*. He was close to sealing the Columbia deal when Lamar inadvertently played the song for Elvis. He flipped over it and wanted to record it. Eddie had to make the hard decision to keep the song to launch his own recording career, or have the biggest star in the world record it. For the songwriter in him it was a no-brainer. He went for the Elvis cut. It became Elvis's last certified million selling single and put Eddie on the map as a serious songwriter, but it killed his own record deal.

I asked Eddie if he ever got the chance to meet Elvis after *Kentucky Rain* was a hit and he told me that Lamar arranged for him to fly out to Vegas to meet The King during one of his concert tours. Eddie made the trip and that night Lamar escorted him to Elvis's dressing room door, and asked Eddie to wait there while he went to see if it was cool to take him inside. After standing there for about twenty minutes, which Eddie said felt like an hour, the door flew open, Lamar and Elvis appeared, and Lamar said, "Elvis this is Eddie Rabbitt, the man who wrote *Kentucky Rain*." Elvis turned to Eddie and said, with a curled lip, "Nice-a-meet-ya." That was it! Then he was gone! After hearing that story, it was a running gag for Eddie and I. Every time we met someone who acted too big for their britches, we'd turn to each other and say, "Nice-a-meet-ya."

CHAPTER 49

··

My Idaho Girl

Shortly before I sold my properties on Music Row, I hired a real estate agent to handle leasing out some of my buildings. I arrived at his office one day to sign on a new lease for my studio, The Garage. The prettiest girl with the sweetest smile greeted me at the front desk and asked me if I would like some coffee. Well, she brought me more than that, but not until a year later.

I had just come out of another relationship and was enjoying being unattached, with no hurry to get involved again. A year passed and every so often that pretty girl's face would come into my mind. One day I called my friend and asked if she still worked for him. He

Son Luke & Korene.

told me she had moved on, but he thought he still had her phone number. I asked him to see if he could set me up with a date. He did, and I'd like to say she fell head over heals for me immediately, but she was a skeptical sort and it took a while for her to warm up to me.

Korene hailed from Twin Falls, Idaho and came to Nashville to get a degree in Music from Belmont College. She was a fine singer and had traveled the country with a Christian band called Captive Free, spreading the good word from state to state before she came to Nashville. Korene worked her way through college with an assortment of jobs and was about to graduate when I met her. She obviously couldn't resist my charms for long and we fell madly in love, got married in Seaside, Florida in a cute little oceanfront honeymoon cottage with our friends, Sarah and Charlie Modica standing up for us. In 1997 our wonderful son, Luke, was born.

CHAPTER 50

....

Tim McGraw

The freedom gained by loosening up my schedule led to a rash of writing with many old and new co-writers. One of my favorite co-conspirators became Mark Collie. We went on a writing binge that produced some very special songs and significant recordings.

Tim McGraw gave us a great cut of *Carry On*, co-written with Hillary Kanter. It was included on Tim's "A Place In The Sun" album which went on to sell over three million records. Hillary, Mark, and I got the rare pleasure of seeing Tim sing that song from Tim's private box on his New Year's Eve concert at what is now called the Bridgestone Arena in Nashville. It was exciting, and he and his band, the Dance Hall Doctors, nailed the song that night! Tim was his usual cool self and even asked Mark to come on stage and sing our song with him.

Besides getting cuts of our new creations by other artists, Mark Collie also was making some rocking music of his own. He recorded our co-written songs, *Trouble's Comin' Like A Train* and Linda Lou on his MCA album, "Mark Collie" and his next album, "Unleashed" contained our song, *Waiting*, all written by the three of us, Hillary, Mark, and I.

In 1999 Mark starred in the short film, "I Still Miss Someone," directed by John Lloyd Miller. Mark portrayed Johnny Cash during his wild and crazy young years during the time of the Sun recording sessions. Mark's singing and acting was superb and won the Nashville Film Festival Award for Best Film and Best Short Film that year. It was downright spooky how much he sounded and looked like the great Johnny Cash. Everyone thought he should have been chosen to star in the movie, "Walk The Line," which he pursued, but the role went to the established actor, Joaquin Phoenix. I truly believe that Mark would have been spectacular in that roll, probably making the film even more believable. Do yourself a favor and get a copy of Mark's DVD, "I Still Miss Someone". It's fantastic.

In 1998, Patrick Swayze and Randy Travis starred in Black Dog, a movie about a shady side of truck driving, and the theme song became country star Rhett Akins' gritty version of our song, *Drivin' My Life Away*. Rhett and producer Frank Liddell took an electric guitar-slinger approach to the song and I was impressed that they didn't play it safe and try to copy Eddie's version. I attended the big premier they had in Nashville.

CHAPTER 51

....

Losing Eddie Rabbitt

Six days after the Black Dog premier, my great friend and long time partner, Eddie Rabbitt passed away. The family had a very quiet ceremony with close friends and band members. As I stood with my hand on his casket, I was in disbelief, reflecting that I was best man at his marriage to Janine, standing with him the sad day he had to bury his young son Timmy and here I was, helping lay to rest the man I spent twenty-some years around, writing literally hundreds of wonderful songs, sitting thousands of hours in front of studio speakers listening to him sing, recording album after album, and having the ever-loving time of our lives. I've never laughed with someone so much in my life. God bless him and his family.

Someday I'm Gonna Rent This Town

CHAPTER 52

Mom and Dad

If losing Eddie Rabbitt wasn't tough enough, the years between 2000 and 2003 brought on more sad days for me and my family. In 2000 my father passed away from a long bout with cancer that spread throughout his body. Shortly after his death my mother contracted a strange illness called Guillain-Barre Syndrome. They believe it is a condition brought on by influenza shots. I can tell you from experience that I would rather risk getting the flu than have to succumb to this malady. My sister and I spent two years by my mother's side in hospitals in Cleveland, Dayton, and Bellefontaine, Ohio. Our mother, Opal, bless her heart, didn't die from the syndrome, but from the inadequate care she received at a Cleveland hospital. Never have I experienced such unprofessional, egomaniacal doctors, and rude, uncaring nurses. Opal died from lack of care and being in the hospital so long without proper isolation, and months of unnecessary contact with infectious germs. She finally succumbed to her infections in May of 2003, although they had the gall to list the cause of

The picture my Dad carried of my Mom, Opal, all through World War II.

death as heart failure. Those doctors and nurses should be ashamed of themselves and drummed out of the healthcare profession.

CHAPTER 53

....

Alabama

     Right before my father passed away at the turn of the century, the supergroup Alabama surprised Mark Collie, Hillary Kanter, and myself by recording our song, *Small Stuff*. The record was released in late 1999 and was rapidly climbing the Country charts, but suddenly stopped at number 24. We were shocked, and came to find out that the label, as a new millennium gift to prominent radio stations, had sent CD players to them with a CD of another Alabama song, *The Twentieth Century*, on it as celebration of the year 2000 and the turn of the century. The stations mistakenly thought it was a brand new single release by the group and started playing that song instead of ours. That killed our airplay. It was very disheartening because it was a strong release by Alabama and had the potential for being a big chart topper. But as the old song said, "Que Sera Sera . . . whatever will be will be."

     In 2014 I did get the opportunity to sing that song on stage with Alabama's lead singer, Randy Owens and his band in Muscle Shoals, Alabama at his yearly benefit for St. Jude's Children's Hospital. By quirky fate, the publisher of this book, Sherman Smith, was at that show and approached me after I performed and asked me to write this book. As I said, Que Sera Sera.

Someday I'm Gonna Rent This Town

CHAPTER 54

Surprise, Surprise, Surprise

It's always a welcome and unexpected gift when someone records your song without you knowing it or asking them to. I discovered that rock's Elvis Costello had recorded *Put 'em All Together (I'd Have You)*, originally recorded by the legend, George Jones. What made it even more righteous was the fact that it was a live recording done at a performance at L.A.'s funky and famous Palomino Club.

Out of the blue, another surprise! I found out that the British rasta supergroup, Steel Pulse, had recorded a version of *When You're In Love With A Beautiful Woman*. They got down on it and their rendition has become one of my favorite recordings of that song.

CHAPTER 55

More Surprises

In 2004 I got a call from my friend, Paul Overstreet, telling me that a song we wrote twenty-five years before had been recorded by the then up-and-coming country artist, Blake Shelton, on his new album "Blake Shelton's Barn & Grill." That news was just what I needed to get back in the swing of life and away from the previous hard years.

Songwriter and producer Bobby Braddock, and engineer friend Ed Seay made one hell of a fine sounding record of our song- *Cotton Pickin' Time,* and Blake really sold the story of a country boy making good in love and business. I love it when it comes together as hot as that in the recording studio, thanks to musicians Shannon Forrest, Glenn Worf, Frank DeBretti Jr., Paul Franklin, Tim Lauer, Terry McMillan, Mike Rojas, Brent Rowan, Jonathan Yudkin, and Background vocals by Paul Overstreet and Melodie Crittenden.

Someday I'm Gonna Rent This Town

CHAPTER 56

Ripoff or What?

Imagine my surprise when I received an e-mail from EMI Music Publishing, the publisher of my song *When You're In Love With A Beautiful Woman*, informing me that three of their international songwriters took the hook from my song and wrote a brand new song simply called *Beautiful Woman*! They said it was an "interpolation" of my song, a term totally unknown to me after all these years in the business. Frankly, the word "plagiarism" more quickly came to mind.

Perturbed, I phoned the publisher and they explained that their writers took it upon themselves to use my hook, melody and lyric, and that the song they wrote was already recorded by an up-and-coming urban artist from Australia by the name of Kyle. They needed my permission to use it as his new single release. Without committing myself, I told them to send me a copy of the record and I, or my attorney, would get back to them.

Much to my surprise, I enjoyed what they did with the extensive use of my hookline and title. But, I knew that if they released the song and it became a hit, it would be the end of any chance I would have for someone to record my original song for a very long time. Therefore I informed them of what conditions I would allow them to use my song title and hook.

They agreed to my terms and mixed four different dance versions by various producers and guest hip-hop artists, and it became a popular dance song in Australia.

Someday I'm Gonna Rent This Town

CHAPTER 57

Tim McGraw Strikes Again!

For nearly ten years, various musician friends would tell me stories concerning Tim McGraw and his interest in our song, *Suspicions*. They said at recording sessions, while working out songs with the studio players, Tim would play *Suspicions* and say, "One day I'm going to record that song." Others would relate that he would sometimes play it in his dressing room before a concert.

In 2007 it happened. Tim's production, along with Darran Smith and Byron Galimore, was awesome and the album, "Let It Go" entered the Billboard 200 at number one with sales of 325,000 copies. There were seven single releases from the album and it became certified multi-platinum. The video of *Suspicions* was shot live at one of Tim's sold out concerts, and it had a great run on CMT, GAC and other video television programs. *Suspicions* lyric is all about being in love with a woman that turned heads everywhere she goes. For Tim, his beautiful wife, Faith Hill maybe? It was a perfect fit and rose to number twelve on the Country charts and into the 1980's in the Pop Charts.

Someday I'm Gonna Rent This Town

CHAPTER 58

Writin' My Life Away

Shortly after that release, Scotty Emerick, Paul Overstreet, and I got together and wrote a song I believe is one of the best songs I've ever been a part of. I'd had the title for *Long Story Short* for a couple of years and tried my best to write a song around it, but always came up short in my expectations. I knew the hook, "To Make a *Long Story Short*, She's gone," was special and worthy of a great song but was never satisfied with the outcome.

I showed up for our writing session at the agreed upon time to find Scotty Emerick sitting there playing his beat up gut string acoustic guitar. I tuned my guitar up and showed him the idea I had been toiling with for so long. Within minutes, Scotty began playing an unusual soulful riff to go with it and shortly we had the makings of something magic. Paul then arrived and loved what we had so far and I suggested that we make the verses rather complicated and wordy so that when we capped it with the simple, "To make a *Long Story Short*, she's gone," it would have the desired effect. Paul came up with just the right approach, both lyrically and melody wise. It wasn't long before we had it and taking a celebratory selfie to tack up on the office wall.

A few weeks later Paul heard that Kenny Chesney was looking for material for a new album and played the song for him and he recorded it. As they say, it's "in the can" and we're hoping he will release it someday soon.

While we've been waiting for that day, Kenny Chesney has

graced Paul, Scotty, and I with another recording that is on his album, "Hemingway's Whiskey." This song, *Round and Round*, was written and demoed at my studio, the Camp Overlook Recording Spa. Kenny and his producer Buddy Cannon made a robust version of our song about the way some people never seem satisfied with their particular lot in life.

CHAPTER 59

The Originals

I've always been in awe and have great respect for the first recordings, or demonstration tapes, that are usually made once a songwiter or songwriters finish a tune. They have such fire and enthusiasm in their sound and are perfect examples of the way the songs were conceived and meant to be heard. The renditions range from simple guitar or keyboard and vocal to full-blown orchestrations. Sometimes, when that song is pitched and cut by a recording artist, it reaches creative and sonic heights way beyond your wildest dreams. Sometimes it faithfully copies the original demo and sometimes, sadly, it misses the mark completely. As a songwriter, when you give permission to use your song, that's always the gamble you take.

Years ago I began collecting my favorite demo recordings by my favorite songwriters with the idea of someday presenting them to the world. I always felt that it was a shame the public never heard these wonderful works of art, they just sit on publisher's shelves, seemingly of no use to anyone. Far from that, these recordings are musical history. These are the sketches that Rembrandt made before painting the masterpiece that we all know. These demoes are inspiration personified.

From amassing hundreds of original demos, I find that many times the original becomes my favorite version of the popular song. Often it is not the amount of money spent on a master recording that makes it top the songwriter's first version. The purity of the excitement, love, and cherished approach that the composer "gets on tape" has a magic that, in some ways, can never be surpassed.

Additionally, there are renditions of songs sung by the songwriters that speak volumes to the fact that the world has been cheated out of the pleasure of hearing some truly wonderful singers, be it at their own choosing or only because they fell victim to the recording business's crazy crap game and just had a bad roll of the dice. A few voices come to mind: Richard Leigh, Hugh Prestwood, Scotty Emerick, Gretchen Peters, John Reynolds, Laura Vida, Leslie Satcher, and Rebecca Lynn Howard. Thankfully these singer/songwriters are still producing songs and very much in the game. Here's hoping their superb voices get to be heard by the masses in the very near future.

With all the above in mind, I have taken it upon myself to produce and host a radio show called, "The Originals – Inside the World of Songwriting." Each one hour episode features nine or ten original versions by the songwriter or songwriters who wrote them and some history about their creation. Occasionally I do short interviews with the writers about their particular song that's featured as well. The entire original version is always played and at times, I segue into the popular artist's version if it's especially interesting and special. At the time of this writing, "The Originals" runs every Sunday night in Nashville, Tennessee on Hippie Radio/94.5FM at 8 pm, Central Time. It can be heard online in real time by clicking on "listen to it live" at Hippie Radio Nashville.

CHAPTER 60

....

Songwriter Festivals

When I first moved to Nashville with hopes of becoming a professional songwriter, I played my songs live at every opportunity. Thankfully, there were a handful of clubs, restaurants, and listening venues in Music City, and passing the hat kept me in Kraft macaroni and cheese and Jiffy corn bread for a couple of years. Who needs much of anything else when you have a dream?

As I began to have some success as a songwriter, I became busier and busier with pitching appointments, recording sessions and all that goes with advancing the career. The live performances began to take second place and, eventually I stopped playing my songs live at all.

Then one day, I got a call from my friend Paul Overstreet. He was hosting an annual benefit concert for St. Jude's Hospital at the Hard Rock Theater in Biloxi, Mississippi. He asked me to come down and play my songs for the folks, and I remember saying, "No one wants to hear me sing those songs." He assured me that they would, and that performing again would be loads of fun..... I've been playing concerts, Songwriter's festivals and private parties ever since. It is such a grand experience every time the audience sings along to *I Love A Rainy Night, Love Will Turn You Around* or *When You're In Love With A Beautiful Woman.*

I don't know why I was blessed to have this wonderful experience of writing songs for a living, but I realize how lucky I am and never take it for granted. The bonus of meeting and having great friends whose talents just blow me away is an indescribable joy.

So come see me next time I'm in your neck of the woods. I love seeing those smiling faces out there in audiences everywhere from Key West, Florida to Crested Butte, Colorado, Whitefish, Montana to Coeur d'Alene, Idaho., The Virgin Islands to Martha's Vineyard, Indian Lake, Ohio and every town in between.

I hope to see your smiling face too real soon.

CHAPTER 61

....

Songwriting Tips

Songwriting 101-1

I do believe that anyone has the potential to write a song . . . now, a "Hit" song, I'm not so sure.

When I arrived in Nashville, I had a handful of tunes that I thought should be on the radio, not a doubt in my mind. Not too long ago, I came upon some cassette tapes of those songs from my first pitches to producers and A & R people at the various labels, and I was amazed! Not at the quality of the songs, but at the fact that I really thought they stood a chance in those days. I noticed that more than half of them were so esoteric that while listening now, I don't have a clue what I was even trying to say in those songs! If I can't understand what I was saying, how in the world did I ever think that someone like George Jones was going to record them? What a dreamer I was!

Of course, being a dreamer was exactly what I had to be, or I would have never been self-assured enough to stick it out and learn the craft of songwriting. More important, you have to be smart and realize that something is missing that make people connect to your songs. I came to realize that one of those missing pieces was plain language, and lyrics that spoke to the listener in a direct everyday way. Conversational lyrics, much like you would talk to your best friend . . . no frills, no complicated words, just to the point and clearly stated. When I started approaching my songs that way, things started opening up for me in Nashville.

Songwriting 101-2

Once I had a few hits under my belt, new writers would look me up for advice. Sitting with someone who wants my honest opinion about their songs, is not one of my favorite things to do. I really hate to discourage anyone or step on their dreams, or lie to them for that matter, just to avoid hurting their feelings.

Usually, I start these meetings with these words. "You can write a song and play it for your friends and relatives, and they may think it's just the greatest song they ever heard, and that's super! There is absolutely nothing wrong with that, and it's valid and worthwhile.

On the other hand, if you want to make a living writing songs, you have to remember that there are no guarantees. You may have the most unbelievable songs ever written and never have any success. I like to use Vincent Van Gogh as an example. That poor fellow painted such unique and interesting paintings and never made over eight dollars in his career! Now, his paintings are priceless.

If you are looking for camaraderie, a creative and interesting way of life, songwriting can give you all those things. But, if you are looking for a sure thing, songwriting is not it.

Songwriting 101-3

You must be obsessed to make it in Nashville as a songwriter. They estimate that 20 to 30 new hopeful songwriters come to town each week, and most of them leave within a month. I don't know where that statistic comes from, but from my observations that sounds about right.

Many think that there is a "click" in Nashville, that there is some sort of unofficial club you need to be a part of to get anywhere with your songs. There is no "click," you just have to be here for a long time, playing at every open mike night you can, meeting every publisher you can wrangle an appointment with, writing with other songwriters and just be a "presence." The music community becomes aware of you and gradually starts taking you seriously. Perhaps, if you're lucky, one of your tunes gets a reputation for it's uniqueness, quality or quirkiness . . . your name becomes familiar to their ears.

Songwriting 101-4

You can't do it alone. I wondered around Music Row for two years before I met my mentor, Jim Malloy. He gave me direction, encouragement, and faith that I could make it. He saw past my flaws and weaknesses as a songwriter and supported me financially, emotionally, and letting me experiment and grow in my talents. It will all come together for you more easily and professionally if you have a wise sage on your side.

Songwriting 101-5

They say in sports, always compete with someone who is better than you. That goes for co-writing as well. Always try to co-write with people who have some skills or style that is better or different from your own. Quite often you will end up with a creation that neither one of you would have written alone . . . something unique.

Songwriting 101-6

If you are making recordings of your songs at home, here's a tip from my mentor, Jim Malloy, one of the most famous and awarded recording engineers in the world. The microphone is like the human ear. Place the microphone where the signal being recorded sounds best to your own ear. For example, listen to the guitar at different positions and distances and place the microphone at the position that sounds the best.

Songwriting 101-7

Write about what every person feels. Admit your human weaknesses and fears, and other people will relate to your song.

Songwriting 101-8

Whatever you do . . . don't be boring!

Someday I'm Gonna Rent This Town

CHAPTER 62

....

What I've Learned Along the Way -
Advice from Great Hall of Fame Songwriters

1. Hugh Prestwood - *(The Song Remembers When,*
Ghost in This House, On The Verge)

It took a while in my songwriting growth before I began to understand that I wasn't only writing songs to turn on myself, but was also writing them to turn on someone I'd never met. I then began to mentally bring that unknown listener into my writing room. I started trying to grasp what I might say – musically and lyrically – that (a) deeply moved me, and (b) would move this complete stranger as well. Finding this psychic/emotional common ground between the two of us was, and still is, my magic key to unlocking those doors which – occasionally, anyway – open up to reveal great, meaningful songs.

2. Gretchen Peters - *(Independence Day, The Secret of Life,*
On A Bus To St. Cloud)

If you are "stuck" on a line or with a particular part of a song, take a nap. Sleep (and the time just before you fall asleep) puts your brain into a different state. Your subconscious takes over and works out problems – if you've ever gotten stuck on a crossword puzzle, taken a quick nap and woke up with the solution you know how this works. Alternately, take a walk. Anything to stop your conscious mind from attacking the problem and "letting" your subconscious play with it. Your subconscious is your co-writer!

3. Paul Overstreet - *(When You Say Nothing At All, Forever & Ever Amen, Some Beach)*

The more you write the more you know you can. And, as you go into a writing appointment, you will go in with the expectations of getting a great song. Chances are, with that attitude, you will.

4. Richard Leigh - *(Don't It Make My Brown Eyes Blue, Life's Highway, The Greatest Man I Never Knew)*

My biggest songs always came out sounding so simple, but simple is hard.

5. Roger Cook - *(I Believe In You, Long Cool Woman (In A Black Dress), I'd Like To Teach The World To Sing)*

To earn a 'living' most songwriters have to listen to what the radio is playing, and try to emulate those hit's. This can put you on the fast track to monetary success, and, lets face it, money is very attractive ! But, unless one strives to be original now and again, and reach inside for something a little deeper, you'd better look out for something else to do when your time as 'flavour of the month' has passed. I would suggest, for every two song's you write strictly for the popular medium of the day, you write one for your soul. And, if your lucky, just once in a while you might come up with something both thoughtful and melodic that against most odd's, becomes a 'hit', one which opens the door to a richer bounty, a lifelong, heart sustaining career.

6. Layng Martine - *(The Greatest Man I Never Knew, Rub It In, Way Down)*

Start with three songs you love, at least two of which are at least thirty years old or so . . . songs that have stood the test of time.

On a clean sheet of paper, write down the lyrics to each song BY HAND. Then write three new songs, one in the exact same form as each one of the three songs you love . . . with lines the same length, rhymes in the same places and the overall song the same number of verses and choruses and bridges as the song you love.

You will begin to see how hit songs are constructed, how quickly the stories are told and how quickly a great lyric "cuts to the chase" and makes its point.

Once you're thoroughly at home and familiar with the form and brevity of songs you love you'll be much more able to construct new forms of your own in addition to using classic, proven forms if you want to.

CHAPTER 63

....

I Believe

Stupid people shouldn't breed.
Most people think the singer wrote the song.
Our American culture is far too politically correct.

To paraphrase George Carlin:
Some people are Stupid,
Some People are Crazy,
Some people are Full of Shit... Some People Are All Three!

CHAPTER 64

....

Artist Who Have Recorded Even Stevens Songs

Eddie Rabbitt

I Love A Rainy Night
Drivin' My Life Away
Suspicions
Step By Step
Someone Could Lose A Heart Tonight
You Can't Run From Love
Pour Me Another Tequila
Gone Too Far
Do You Right Tonight
Warning Sign
The Best Year Of My Life
B-B-B-Burnin' Up With Love
I Just Want To Love You
Song Of Ireland
She's Coming Back To Say Goodbye
I Can't Help Myself
We Can't Go On Living Like This
Hearts On Fire
Drinkin' My Baby (Off Of My Mind)
I Should Have Married You
Rhonda
Could've Been Somebody Else
Big Brown Eyes
Forgive & Forget
Long Gone
It Just Ain't Hit Me Yet

Leavin'
I Can't Get This Ring Off My Finger
There's Someone She Lies To
Stop Look & Listen
The Girl On My Mind
Sure Thing
She Loves Me Like She Means It
Good Night For Falling In Love
Our Love Will Survive
Bedroom Eyes
Laughin' On The Outside
All My Life, All My Love
Bring Back The Sunshine
Skip-A-Beat
Dim,Dim The Lights
Rivers
My Only Wish
Every Night I Fall In Love With You
Go To Sleep Big Bertha
So Fine
I Will Never Let You Go Again
Amazing Love
Short Road To Love
Rockin' With My Baby
I Need To Fall In Love Again
So Deep In Your Love
Pretty Lady

What Will I Write
Just The Way It Is
A World Without Love
1-2-3 (You Really Got A Hold On Me)
Dial That Telephone

Engelbert Humperdinck
What Will I Write
I Don't Know How To Say Goodbye
Beautiful Baby
Patiently Waiting
You Look Good On Me
Two Lovers
Stay With Me Stay
Meet Me In Memphis

Dolly Parton
It's Such A Heartache

Ricky Skaggs
Lovin' Only Me

Sammi Smith
I'm In For Stormy Weather
The Days That End In "Y"
Paste Me On Some Feathers
I Was Just Fifteen
Good For Something Years
Darlin' It's Good To Have You Home
Huckelberry Pie
Fine As Wine
I'll Get Bette r
Good Morning Sunshine, Goodbye
Go Easy On My Heart
You Got The Power

Elvis Costello
Put 'em All Together (I'd Have You)

Lacy J. Dalton
Black Coffee
Forever In My Heart
Rainman
Lay A Little Love On Me
Don't Try To Tell Me Nothin's Goin'
On
Turn To A Little 3rd Rate Romance
Lonesome (As The Night Is Long)
Shaky Ground
That Road
Stay With Me

The Oak Ridge Boys
No Matter How High
A Little Love Can Go A Long Long
Way
Stay With Me Stay

Hillary Kanter
We Work
Crazy In Love
It's Such A Heartache
Good Night For Falling In Love
Dreamers Like Us
Someday You'll Love Me
Ain't It A Good Day
The Fool In The Rearview Mirror
Blue On Blue
Rainy Day Blues
Early Morning Memories
Black Coffee
The Right One
Soul Searchin'
Lonesome Road
Love Letters At Midnight
Much Better Off
Baby Won't Do It

Without You
The Love You Left In Me
California Christmas
My Heart's Saying Yes
I Couldn't Help Myself
I Need To Fall In Love Again

Mac Davis
Somewhere In America
After The Lights Go Down Low

Conway Twitty
It's Such A Heartache
Crazy In Love
When You're In Love With A Beautiful Woman
Someday You'll Love Me

George Jones
Put 'em All Together (I'd Have You)

Julio Iglasias
Crazy In Love

Kyle
Beautiful Woman

The Chipmuncks
I Love A Rainy Night

Joe Cocker
Crazy In Love

Tom Jones
I Love A Rainy Night

Ronnie McDowell
Cotton Pickin' Time
When You're In Love With A Beautiful Woman

Micky Gilly & Charly Mcclain
The Phone Call

Jim Ed Brown & Helen Cornielus
All The Time In The World

Stonewall Jackson
Don't Be Late

Chris Ladoux
Fine As Wine

Amanda Stott
Black Is Black

Blake Shelton
Cotton Pickin' Time

Kenny Chesney
Long Story Short
Round & Round

Martina McBride
A Great Disguise

Marie Osmond
99% Of The Time

Tim McGraw
Carry On
Suspicions

Roger Miller
Key West Skies

Trace Adkins
When I Stop Loving You

Alabama
Small Stuff

Stella Parton
Room At The Top Of The Stairs
Danger Of A Stranger
Four Little Letters
Easy To Love
It's The Little Things
Long Lost Love
Someone
A Little Inconvenient
Honey Come Home
I Cried For The Lady

Billy Mize
Put'em All Together (I'd Have You)

Barbara Mandrell
I Love A Rainy Night

Crystal Gayle
99% of the Time

Suzy Bogguss
Blue Days

Steel Pulse
When You're In Love With A Beautiful
Woman

Marilyn Mccoo
Two Lovers

Mark Collie
Trouble's Comin' Like A Train
Linda Lou
Waiting

Kim Carnes
Crazy In Love

Rhett Akins
Drivin' My Life Away

Kathy Mattea
Crazy In Love

Bob Gibson
Killed By A Coconut

Billy Burnett
You Leave It Up To Me

McBride & The Ride
Your One & Only

Bill Purcell Orchestra
When You're In Love With A Beautiful
Woman

Kenny Rogers
Love Will Turn You Around
Crazy In Love

Sweet Pea Atkinson & Was (Not Was)
Suspicions

B.J. Thomas
I Don't Know How To Say Goodbye

Dr. Hook
When You're In Love With A Beutiful Woman
S.O.S. For Love
The Shadow Knows
Loveline
All The Time In The World
In Over My Head
What Do You Want
I Want Johnny's Job
Angela's Eyes
Before The Tears
Do You Right Tonight

Yvonne Elliman
This Lonliness

Paul Overstreet
Beautiful Baby

Billy Joe Royal
The Real Thing

Johnny Lee
The 13th of July

J.D. Souther
Looks Like It's Gonna Rain Today

The London Symphony
When You're In Love With A Beautiful Woman

CHAPTER 65

··

Even Stevens Songs in Movies and TV

Love Will Turn You Around / Kenny Rogers - "Six Pack"
Drivin My Life Away / Rhett Akins - "Black Dog"
Drivin My Life Away / Eddie Rabbitt - "The Roadie"
Drivin My Life Away / TV series "The Americans"
I Love A Rainy Night / Eddie Rabbitt - Yoplait Yogurt Commercial
Round and Round / Kenny Chesney - TV series "Dallas"
I Love A Rainy Night / Eddie Rabbitt - Miller Beer Commercial
Drivin My Life Away / Eddie Rabbitt - The Night Rider
I Love A Rainy Night / Grand Theft Auto (video game)
The A Team
Cracker (BBC America)
Fall Guy
Jenny Jone Show
Knight Rider
One of Our Aircraft Is Missing
Today Show
Days of Our Lives
Teenage Dreams
Donny & Marie - Behind the Music
Best of American Bandstand
Divorcing Jack
De Kampioenen
America Country Hits
Barbara Mandrell and the Mandrell Sisters
America's Funniest Home Videos
Big Breakfast
Century Of Country

Crook & Chase
Hello Darlin - A Tribute to Conway Twitty
Life & Times of Ralph Stanley
Monday Night Concerts
Old Folks Downhome
Prime Time Country
Statler Bros. Show
This Week In Country Music
Today's Country
Video Morning
33rd Academy of Country Music Awards
Ed
Hit List
Jam Zone
Monday Night Concerts
Kidsongs Tv
KMBC News at 4
KSL News at 10
Access Hollywood
ACM Preview 98
Lou Hobbs Show
VH1 Solid Gold